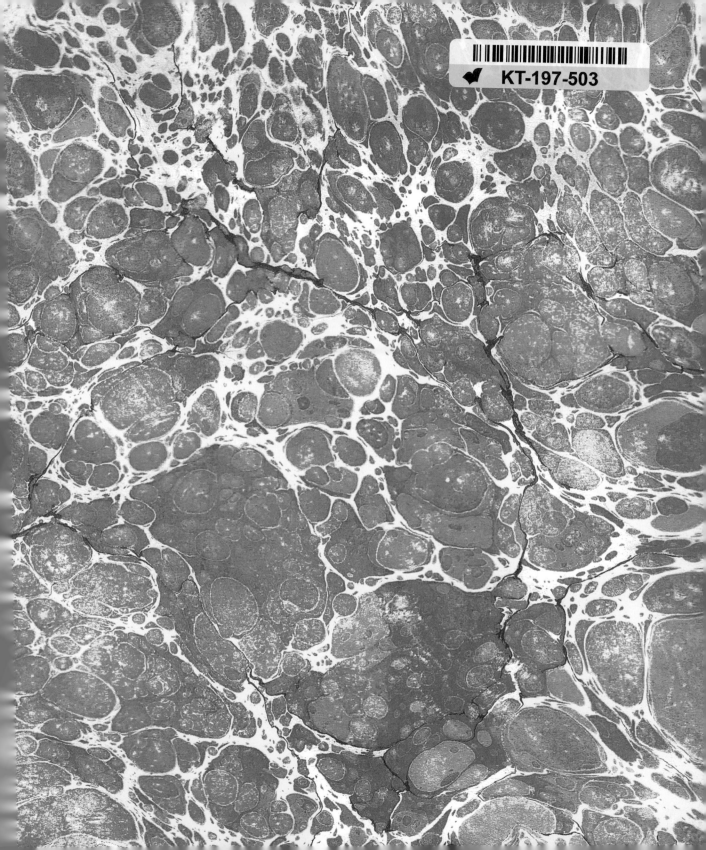

COCKTAILS

with

BOMPAS & PARR

Dear Jim & Kate,

Merry Christmas,

Love Nutto

xxxxx
xx

PAVILION

Xmas 2011

First published in the United Kingdom in 2011 by
PAVILION BOOKS
10 Southcombe Street, London W14 0RA

An imprint of Anova Books Company Ltd

Associate Publisher: Nina Sharman
Designer: Georgina Hewitt
Editor: Maggie Ramsay
Proofreader: Barbara Dixon
Photographer: Beth Evans (except for pages below)
Stylists: Lightning & Kinglyface

ISBN: 978-1-86205-906-1

A CIP catalogue record for this book is available from the British Library.

10 9 8 7 6 5 4 3 2 1

Reproduction by Dot Gradations Ltd, UK
Printed and bound by 1010 Printing International Ltd., China

The authors would like to thank the following people for providing photographs:
p.7 Nathan Pask, p.17 Barney Steel, p.18 Dan Price, pp.22–3 Ann Charlotte Ommedal,
p.28 Chloe Thacker, p.98 Barney Steel pp.148, 150, 153, 155 Andrew Stellitano,
p.160 Ben Ottewels

www.anovabooks.com

CONTENTS

Introduction 6
Our Top 10 Drinking Stories 8
Universal Cocktail Principles 14
Types of Cocktails 20
Basic Equipment 26

RECIPES

Classics
Gin Cocktails 34
Whisk(e)y Cocktails 40
Rum Cocktails 46
Vodka Cocktails 52
Tequila Cocktails 56
Brandy Cocktails 60
Champagne Cocktails 66

Our Favourites
Galactic Booze 74
Buckfast 76
Black Velvet 80
Getting Drunk on the Cheap 82
Absinthe 84
Ether Cocktail 86

Old & Obscure
Children & Alcohol 90
Captain Fraser 92
Royal Usquebaugh 94
Soyer au Champagne 96

Punches & Party Drinks

Architectural Punch Bowl 100

Emperor's Shrub 102

Fish House Punch 104

True Friendship Punch 106

Black Gin Punch 108

Eggnog 110

Ginger Beer 112

Citronade 114

Futurist Cocktail 114

Cures

Bullshot 118

Evelyn Waugh's Noonday Reviver 118

Langan's Elixir 120

Fernet Branca 122

Hanky Panky 123

Tobacco Elixir 124

Techniques

Glasses 130

Garnishes 131

Flaming 134

Infusions 136

Eggs 140

Foams 142

Ice Cream 145

Bar Snacks

Bacon Frazzles 148

Scratchings 149

Bacon Popcorn 150

Curried Crab 151

Quail Cottage 152

Marshmallows 154

Suppliers 156

Bibliography 157

Index 158

Honour Roll 160

INTRODUCTION

Alcohol is the universal drug. Most cultures have enjoyed a millennia-long affair with drink, using it medically, socially and as a means to explore the mystical. It helps humanity communicate with God through the Eucharist; inspires artists like Jackson Pollock to create beauty; and contributes to the joy of being alive.

The dark side makes it all the more interesting. Prohibitionists tell us that it is a blight on society and has led to every imaginable vice. A lot of people find it inspiring. The power of alcohol is indicated in the vast amounts of cash generated by the drinks industry. A single brewer, AB InBev (home of Stella Artois and Beck's), listed revenues of 36.8 billion USD in 2009. This is almost twice what the US government spends on its space programme annually.

This book is an alcoholic adventure, exploring the physical, ethical, architectural, social and historical dimensions of drinks and cocktails. We want to totally blow away the mystique and pretensions associated with cocktails. Along the way you'll learn to make some cracking drinks.

Bompas & Parr has worked on a number of alcohol-inspired projects. We have created a dense cloud of breathable Hendrick's Gin and tonic that allowed you to become intoxicated through your lungs and eyeballs. The mist was so thick that you couldn't see friends a metre away. We used doctors as our mixologists to make sure the ratio of gin to tonic was safe and we worked with explosives expert Dr Andrea Sella to make sure the vaporized gin didn't ignite. We've made punch for 25,000 people, in a punch bowl so big that visitors rafted across it before having a glass.

In this book we'll show how to make the perfect Martini, recreate some drinks fit for heroes and investigate booze with fire safety issues. Along the way there are beer floods, alcoholic foams and some fearful hangover cures. And we explore cocktails on a galactic scale, touring the methanol clouds of Sagittarius B_2N and looking forward to drinking in space.

OUR TOP 10 DRINKING STORIES

Rather than embark on a history of cocktails – no one can agree on when, where or how cocktails originated – we present some of the top drink-fuelled moments since the dawn of time. We find them pretty inspiring. How do your drinking stories measure up?

10. LORD BYRON'S BOOT (LATE 18TH CENTURY)

Today most people drink from a glass, some from a tankard and the less tasteful from a coconut or a hollowed-out pineapple. Byron drank from a shoe. This was no ordinary shoe – Byron's flamboyant eccentricity extended to his taste in drinking vessels. Byron's boot was black leather with a silver inscribed rim, a silver spur and heel cap, and a pointed toe for a handle. Byron bought the boot from his mother's side of the family: it was originally given to George Gordon in 1599 and had been passed down the generations.

9. DIANA DEATH JELLY (1997)

One of the most macabre stories to come out of Princess Diana's tragic death. Apparently, a funeral technician working on Diana's death mask used it to make a vodka jelly of her face. Interestingly, moulded and figurative food has played an important role in funerals of the past. Historically, funeral cakes were made using metal, wood and ceramic moulds with motifs including the three plumes that decorate hearses, roosters (symbolizing resurrection) and Masonic symbols.

8. PUSS AND MEW: GIN VENDING MACHINES (EARLY 18TH CENTURY)

As the prices of beer and wine rose in the early 18th century, gin became the drink of choice for Londoners. Parliament passed numerous acts intended to curb the binging and drunken debauchery that followed. But these Gin Acts did little to stop Dudley Bradstreet, who evaded the mandatory Gin Licence by inventing a cunning way to sell gin licence-free on the street. He created what is perhaps the first-ever vending machine. It was marked by the sign of a cat on the wall; passers-by put coins in a slot, uttered *"Puss! Give me two pennyworth of gin"*, held their cup to the spout until they heard the murmur of *"Mew!"* and out came the gin. Since this early prototype, vending machines have sold a wide array of goods, from umbrellas and flowers in Japan to life insurance in American airports; sadly, the gin spouts are a thing of the past.

7. AMERICAN CONSTITUTION (1787)

Signed on 17 September 1787, the American Constitution is one of the most famous documents ever written. Gladstone described it as *"the most wonderful work ever struck off at a given time by the brain and purpose of man"* and after the final signature was added, the 42 delegates got stuck into their next project: a celebration of epic proportions. Swigging and slurring their way through 54 bottles of Madeira, 60 bottles of claret, 22 bottles of port, 8 bottles of whisky, 8 bottles of hard cider, 12 beers and 7 bowls of alcoholic punch large enough for ducks to swim in, the men earned themselves a place in drinking history.

6. A CIVILIZATION BUILT ON BEER (2580 BC)

Few people realize that the Great Pyramid of Giza, like the other pyramids of Egypt, owes its construction to beer. Labourers in Ancient Egypt were paid a minimum wage, measured in beer. A day's labour was rewarded with two containers of the brew. Some historians say Egyptian beer was brewed from bread (cut up into tiny pieces) and flavoured with dates: a very different taste to that drunk today.

5. WINE BY THE FOUNTAIN (1520)

Not one to do things by half, Henry VIII's court consumed an annual 1240 oxen, 8200 sheep, 2330 deer, 760 calves, 1870 pigs, 53 wild boar and over 600,000 gallons of beer. In addition to this, Henry VIII drank wine by the fountain – quite literally. At his lavish feasts, wine cascaded down a 4-metre tall structure for all to drink. In April 2010 historians recreated Henry VIII's octagonal wine fountain in the courtyard of Hampton Court Palace. Based on a well-known painting of the Field of the Cloth of Gold and archaeological excavations, the fountain's exterior is an exact replica but today's fountain uses modern pumps to keep the wine flowing. While the fountain spouts water on weekdays, at the weekend guests can buy a glass of red wine for a small cost. The modern replica is less likely to be surrounded by drunken visitors, but still, as the fountain's motto says: *"faicte bonne chere quy vouldra!"* (let he who wishes make good cheer!).

4. QUAFF FOR YOUR CITY! (1631)

In 1631 the future of a small German city depended on the ability of its citizens to guzzle their drinks. During the Count of Tilly's siege of Rothenburg ob der Tauber, Tilly offered to pardon the city if any of its residents could drink a tankard of wine in one continuous draft. This was no small feat — the tankard he presented held over 3 litres (5¼ pints) of wine! One man, Mayor Nusch, honoured his people and astonishingly completed the task, saving the city from destruction. Unfortunately the mayor slept in a drunken stupor for the next three days, missing the celebrations, but a well-known Bavarian play, *Der Meistertrunk* (The Master Draft), and a daily clock performance in Rothenburg still commemorate his efforts today.

3. PICKLED NELSON (1805)

Horatio Nelson won the Battle of Trafalgar but lost his life in the battle; he returned triumphant but pickled in a barrel of brandy. The ship's supplies provided the most suitable preservative for the Vice Admiral during his final journey back to England. After several weeks at sea, the cargo was unloaded and the body was found to be in perfect condition — although legend has it that there was no brandy in the barrel. Liquor rations had been cut back on the return journey, but the disgruntled sailors demanded drink: *"your Lordships Petitioners were Served out no provisions or liquor of any kind not even their Allowance of wine!"*. The thirsty crew had seemingly drunk every drop from the barrel, giving rise to the phrase "tapping the Admiral".

2. THE WORLD'S LARGEST PUNCH BOWL (1694)

Four hogsheads of brandy, 1 pipe of Malaga wine, 20 gallons of lime juice, 2,500 lemons, 13 hundredweight of fine white sugar, 5 pounds' weight of grated nutmegs, 300 toasted biscuits, 8 hogsheads of water, 6,000 guests and a marble fountain. As commander of the Mediterranean fleet, based in Alicante, British Lord Admiral Edward Russell concocted the world's largest punch...and it was to be more than 300 years before his record was broken – by Bompas & Parr in London in 2010. Unable to find a punch bowl large enough, Russell sought inspiration in his garden and settled on a fountain to serve his colossal brandy punch at an officers' party. Small boys served drinks from wooden canoes, paddling through the punch for only 15 minutes at a time lest they were overcome by the fumes. Guests took a week to drink the fountain dry. The only pause in the celebrations was when it started to rain and a silk canopy was erected to stop the punch from being watered down.

1. THE BEER FLOOD OF 1814

On 17 October 1814 the streets of London were flooded with dark ale following a tidal wave of the brew. Meux's Horse Shoe Brewery of Tottenham Court Road once stood on the site of what is now the Dominion Theatre. A gigantic vat 22ft (6.7m) tall and 60ft (18m) in diameter and big enough to hold 4,000 barrels of beer was built to trump rival brewers. The ale had been maturing for many months when one of the 29 supporting hoops snapped, followed by another, then another. The vat exploded and triggered a domino effect of rupturing beer vats, releasing a tidal wave of over 600,000 litres (132,000 gallons) of beer. Buildings crumbled and innocent people were swept away: the death toll at the scene reached nine. Rescue attempts were further thwarted as thousands of thirsty Londoners packed the streets, scrambling for free drink. But the chaos didn't stop there – further riots broke out in hospitals, where other patients caught scent of the beer-soaked casualties and demanded their fair share. The tragedy was compounded when the dead bodies were exhibited to a paying public. So many people crowded into the room that the floor collapsed and the death toll was pushed higher. Despite efforts to sue the brewery, a judge ruled the event an "Act of God", making this beer flood an official natural disaster.

sweeten drinks. The easiest way to make sugar syrup that we've found is as follows: boil the kettle and, while the water heats, put an empty measuring jug on a pair of scales. Add 100g/3½oz sugar and when the kettle boils add 100ml/3½floz boiling water. Stir to dissolve. Cool and it is ready to use (although using small amounts immediately in a drink won't do too much harm). The syrup will keep for a couple of weeks if stored in the fridge. To make more sugar syrup adjust the quantities in the same 1:1 proportions.

For a longer-lasting syrup you can buy gomme syrup, which is far sweeter and uses gum arabic to stop the sugar crystallizing. But we don't bother; it's just another thing you don't really need.

SHAKING AND STIRRING

Most cocktails need to be either shaken or stirred with ice. The choice of technique depends on the ingredients and the desired texture that you want from the finished drink. Both are easy to master, whatever mixologists may say. Stirring is stirring and shaking is, well, shaking! If you're making lots of cocktails for a party then choose drinks that can be stirred and hence made in quantity, like Martinis, or make a punch that is mixed and iced in its serving dish.

Stirring

Stirring is the right choice for cocktails like Martinis and Sazeracs that are composed of spirits and liqueurs without juices or mixers. A gentle stirring action with large ice cubes will blend and cool the drink while keeping the cocktail smooth and silky. You'll end up with a clean marriage of flavours and a crystal-clear cocktail.

Shaking

Adding citrus juice or fruit to cocktails will naturally make them cloudy, so shaking with ice, which introduces lots of tiny air bubbles into the drink, is a good choice. When you shake a drink the ingredients emulsify together, creating a uniform liquid with a slight froth on top. Adding pineapple juice or a teaspoon of egg white will introduce a lot more froth to a shaken cocktail. Tiny bits of ice will also get incorporated into the drink, which is a real winner when combined with the acidity of many shaken drinks. There is a description of how to use a Boston shaker on pages 26–27.

GLASSES

Choosing the right glass for any given cocktail is paramount. Not least because it may look like you've short-changed your friends if you pour out the drinks and the glasses are only a quarter full. Fortunately, the rules for glassware are straightforward. For short drinks you'll need either cocktail glasses – also known as martini glasses – for serving drinks "straight up" (without ice) or low tumblers, often called "old-fashioned" glasses, for serving drinks "on the rocks" (with ice). For long drinks you need tall, narrow "highball" glasses: they come in various sizes; large ones are better for drinks served with lots of crushed or cubed ice. Champagne flutes are a must for champagne cocktails and, of course, for drinking champagne. Most people have tumblers, highballs and champagne flutes at home; however, it's worth searching for decent glassware as it makes cocktails more enjoyable. Drinking cocktails out of jam jars, while not to be knocked, just doesn't make the drinks taste the same as when sipped from cut crystal. (See also page 130.)

When buying cocktail glasses make sure that they are the right size. For martini-style cocktail glasses it's important that they are not too big: we reckon that glasses that take about 100ml/3½fl oz comfortably are spot on.

Chilling glasses

Cocktails are best when they are extremely cold. The first attack in chilling liquids is to use plenty of decent ice in their preparation. The second is to chill the glasses while you make the drink. There are two ways of doing this. If you put a glass in a freezer for a few minutes it will cool rapidly and become nicely frosted. Alternatively, filling the glass with ice and water, even for a couple of minutes, makes a radical difference. We've heard of bars where they change your glass for a freshly frozen one halfway through your drink, although we suspect that their cocktails must be seriously overpriced if people drink them that slowly!

GARNISHES

We're not talking about a cocktail umbrella in a Pina Colada; garnishes are sometimes an integral part of the drink. Short drinks like Martinis and Sazeracs use strips of lemon and orange peel to introduce further flavour to the drink. The idea is to carefully cut thin strips of peel, squeeze them over the drink to release their aromatic oils, and then either discard the peel or add it to the cocktail. It makes a remarkable difference. You need to use very fresh and unwaxed fruit. Remember that the more you handle fruit the more aromatic oil you'll rub off, so be gentle or cut directly over the glass.

Later in the book we look at some alternative garnishes.

MEASURING

The measures in the recipes are given in parts. We feel that this is best, as it allows you to get a sense of the proportions of the ingredients in each cocktail. Depending on how much you want to drink, what glass you are using and whether the drink is relatively long or short, a "part" is usually between 35 and 70ml/1½ to 2½fl oz — but it's important to use the same part measure within each recipe. It's a good idea to test glasses for size before making a drink, so that you can make the right quantity of cocktail.

Each recipe (except where stated) is for one drink. So when you are making more than one cocktail remember to multiply the other ingredients accordingly.

Types of Cocktails

To demystify cocktails and help you make your own drinks from whatever there is to hand, we have divided the cocktail repertoire into a number of types. These are "sours", "martinis", "old-fashioneds", "punches" and "highballs". Master the idea behind each and it's easy to busk around the theme, substituting alternative spirits and mixers.

SOURS

> *spirit + citrus juice + sugar*

Sours are fun to make, have very few ingredients and taste great. At its most basic a sour could be whiskey with lemon juice and sugar syrup. You can make sours with any spirits but gin and rum will combine with more ingredients than whiskey, brandy or tequila will. Common sours include the Whiskey Sour (bourbon, lemon, sugar) and the Daiquiri (rum, lime, sugar).

You can make variations on sours by replacing the sugar syrup with grenadine syrup or a liqueur like Cointreau or maraschino. The Sidecar (cognac, lemon juice, Cointreau) uses Cointreau to sweeten and balance the cognac and lemon juice as well as introducing orange flavours to the mix. If you use grenadine to sweeten a sour it gives you a Daisy; if you use pineapple juice you'll have made a Fix.

Sugar syrup can be replaced with other types of sweeteners: honey; the bang on trend agave syrup; or even jam. When using a thicker sweetener you need to be careful that you get all the ingredients fully mixed before adding any ice, as the ice can prevent sugars mixing with other ingredients. If you think about the way honey behaves at different temperatures (runny when hot, stiff when cold) you'll get the idea.

There are plenty of other cocktails that are based on sours. Fizzes are sours shaken for an arm-achingly long time, served in a highball glass and topped up with soda water. They should be effervescent when served. Collins are stirred directly in a large highball, iced and topped up with soda water.

When making sours a good rule is to make the spirit between three-quarters and half of the total mix. The sugar and citrus juice are generally added in equal quantity to make up the remainder. However, taste as you go and remember that the strength of lemon and lime juice can vary radically depending on the individual fruit. When you lengthen a sour, turning it into a Fizz or a Collins, you need to add more sugar and citrus, otherwise the cocktail will be lacking in flavour.

MARTINIS

> *spirit + vermouth + bitters*

There's a lot of silly debate among cocktail fiends about where the name "martini" came from, with some implausible stories put forward. Chances are it's derived from the readily available and widely distributed Martini vermouth brand, which is often used in making the drink. Martini-type cocktails are more potent than sours but are filled with subtle flavours. Mixing a spirit like gin with a little vermouth totally transforms the spirit by softening the alcohol and opening up the flavours.

Martinis are made with gin, vermouth and bitters. Simple Martini-style cocktails include the classic Martini (gin, dry vermouth) and the Manhattan (whiskey, sweet vermouth, bitters). Drinks like the Negroni (gin, sweet vermouth, Campari) also fit into this category: Campari is as bitter as anything. If you're so inclined, feel free to apply the term to cocktails made with other liquor bases too. Annoyingly, it now encompasses any cocktail served in a martini glass. There's a big trend for vodka-based Martinis, which you can indulge in at leisure, but you won't find any tips for them here!

Most cocktail books will tell you that a Martini can be adjusted in sweetness by using either Italian (sweet) vermouth, French (dry) vermouth, or a mixture of both for a "perfect" cocktail. It's worth trying different types of vermouth, as the range of flavours is immense.

However, when people ask for a dry Martini they are really commenting on how little vermouth they want in their cocktail, not what type it is. Serious advocates of the dry Martini include Winston Churchill (whose recipe was allegedly to fill a martini glass with iced gin and look at a bottle of vermouth), Kingsley

Amis (who suggested 15 parts gin to 1 part vermouth) and Luis Buñuel ("*ray of sunlight to shine through the bottle of Noilly Prat before it hits the bottle of gin*"). A bar in Spain has a white-clothed altar that is only used for the creation of dry Martinis (quite rightly, it's a splendid drink). The dry Martini is possibly the most effective way to get extreme quantities of alcohol into the blood short of injecting. Handily it comes with a cloak of sophistication.

Properly made Martinis are awesome. Especially if fresh vermouth (try quality brands like Dolin and Noilly Prat) and good gin (Hendrick's, Plymouth, Tanqueray, Sipsmith) are in play. The ratio of spirit to vermouth is anywhere from 2:1 gin to vermouth to perhaps as much as 5:1 if you must have a dry Martini, but any more than that and you are showing off.

One problem might be that people don't properly respect vermouth, the supporting character of the Martini. It is a fortified wine and, like wine, will start to oxidize from the moment you open the bottle. People who despise vermouth might have had a bad experience with old, stale vermouth: this is the destroyer of cocktails. It needs to be fresh. Vermouth is good for a week once opened and will last for a month if kept chilled in the fridge.

Before stirring the gin and vermouth with ice you might add a dash of bitters or liqueur. Keeping everything cold is important with this style of drink, so either bang your glasses in the freezer for a couple of minutes or chuck some iced water into your glass while you mix up the drink.

OLD FASHIONED

spirit + sugar + bitters

If you take any spirit and sip it neat it will often be fairly unpalatable. Adding a little bit of sugar or sugar syrup and a few dashes of bitters to spirits performs a miracle. The classic whiskey Old Fashioned (whiskey, sugar, bitters) mellows out all but the roughest whiskeys and makes them a joy to drink. The Sazerac does the same for cognac or rye whiskey.

PUNCHES

spirit + sweet + sour + weak

This singsong is handy to bear in mind:

One of sour
Two of sweet
Three of strong
Four of weak

Sam learnt it, aged 16, at Notting Hill Carnival and it is pretty versatile. You can slam in anything to hand that fulfils the various criteria and it should work out. You could add some nutmeg and a dash of bitters (Angostura or other bitter spirits, tea or coffee). Then all you need to remember is to chill it.

Make sure you taste your punch to balance it, moderating the "strong" (spirit) with the "weak" (fruit juices, champagne, soda water) and balancing the "sour" (lemon, limes, etc.) and the "sweet" (sugar, honey, liqueurs, jams). Your final punch should be very moreish, the sort of thing guests will drink all night until it takes them by surprise and they realize too late that they are rotted.

HIGHBALLS

> ### *spirit + mixer*

These are not cocktails in the traditional sense of the word. Gin and tonic, although essential from time to time, does not take great dexterity to construct.

Mixers are an easy way to make raw booze taste nicer. Quinine-rich tonic water or fiery ginger beer do wonders to complement the taste of gin or vodka, and more interesting mixers are increasingly appearing on the market. The Fever-Tree range of quality mixers have the decency to be made with real sugar rather than artificial sweeteners.

Mixers themselves have a fascinating history. Coca Cola has been the same for more than a hundred years. It's a true cocktail all on its own and has a taste that is unique, yet when pushed to say what the key ingredients are most people wouldn't have a clue. We once had a jelly emergency right before serving jellies at a Victorian-themed fair. Totally out of ingredients save for Coca Cola, we made Coke jellies but called the dessert a punch jelly cooked up from an original Victorian recipe. The jellies went down a treat; everyone was saying how amazing they tasted. Our guests satisfied and the jellies gone, we made a hasty retreat to our studio: no one realized that our tasty Victorian punch had just a few hours earlier been a bottle of Coke!

BASIC EQUIPMENT

For a great cocktail you need an abundance of decent ice, decent drinking vessels and, most importantly, panache. Equipment doesn't even get a look-in. Of course, it is super helpful to have a few special pieces of kit; without them making cocktails is more time-consuming. With a bit of ingenuity, you'll get by without most of what's listed below, but having the right tools makes things easier.

BOSTON SHAKER

This has two parts: a mixing glass and a metal shaker; they are used individually for mixing drinks and together to form a shaker. You can usually buy both parts together. If not you'll need to take the part that you do have to the shop to check that they fit together. To check that they form a seal, place the metal shaker on top of the glass and tap together using the heel of your hand: when you lift the metal shaker the glass should come with it.

With a little practice the Boston shaker is quicker to use than the "cobbler" shaker — these are all-metal shakers that have a screw-on lid and inbuilt strainer. They come in various sizes and are usually recommended for beginners — but we'd say go with the Boston shaker, the professionals' choice.

If you need to shake a drink in an emergency a Thermos flask works well, although it's hardly glamorous.

Mixing glass

You can mix a "stirred" drink in anything, although having a mixing glass is surprisingly useful: it allows you to get a sense of how much liquid you are putting in if you are not using a measuring device. You'll want to get a 450ml/15fl oz tempered mixing glass that works with a Boston shaker can (see below). It's important that the glass is tempered, as this means it won't crack when subjected to extreme changes in temperature or if you get violent with the ice cubes. It'll be big enough to do a couple of cocktails at a time.

Shaker can

Shaking cocktails with a two-part Boston shaker is easy to master. Always add the ingredients into the mixing glass so that you can get a sense of how much liquid is going in. Don't add ice yet. When all the liquids are in, fill the glass with ice so that it mounds above the brim. Bring down the metal part over the glass and tap it firmly with the heel of your hand to form a seal. To check, lift the metal part slightly and it should bring the glass with it. Turn everything over and tap the glass for good luck. Pick up the shaker with two hands and with the metal part at the bottom shake rapidly and firmly. You can be as wild as you like at this point, but we'd recommend holding with two hands at all times! Shake for about 10 seconds, then place the shaker metal part down on the worktop. To release the seal, hold the shaker in one hand with two fingers wrapped securely around the metal and two around the glass. Then hit the rim of the metal part with the heel of your other hand. The seal may be hard to break because the pressure has built up inside the freezing cold shaker; if it doesn't work, turn the shaker slightly and try again. Persevere and it will release, just don't be tempted to bash it on the worktop.

STRAINERS

If you use a Boston shaker you'll need a strainer to remove ice and other ingredients from your shaken or stirred cocktail.

Hawthorn strainer

This straining device is characterized by a curving spring. It's designed to fit the metal part of a Boston shaker. It's pretty handy and beats using a sieve.

Julep strainer

Looking like a mini colander, this fits inside the glass part of the shaker. It's used for straining stirred drinks. In fact, you can get away without one – the trick is to get a hawthorn strainer that fits your mixing glass snugly. It means it will be a little small for the metal part but will still work.

SPIRIT MEASURE

A spirit measure, or jigger, is important for making consistent drinks. The double-ended type is the most useful: one end measures a *double* and the other a *single*. The actual measure will vary: it all depends on how much booze you want to put in your cocktail. A simple one-spirit cocktail (like an Old Fashioned) will

usually have about 70ml/2½fl oz of liquor. We like using a 35ml/1½fl oz thimble jigger — anything less and your cocktail may not have the desired effect.

POURER

A tapered pourer fits into the bottle with a rubber seal and controls the flow of liquid, whether you are pouring into a measure or just adding a dash of something to your shaker.

BAR SPOON

This has two functions: measuring and stirring. It's like a very long coffee spoon. Not essential — you can "measure" without one, and you can stir with a knife, but your cocktail just won't "taste" as good.

MUDDLER

A mini baseball-bat-shaped pestle designed to crush herbs, fruit and sugar. The best ones are made of wood, although you can get plastic ones. If you don't have one it's not hard to improvise.

KITCHEN KNIFE, PARING KNIFE, PEELER, ZESTER

A kitchen knife is useful for cutting up fruit and making light work of pineapples for adding to punch.

A paring knife is useful for cutting garnishes and peel: be sure to keep it sharp otherwise it's not much use.

A peeler will remove lemon and orange zest thinly and cleanly, leaving the pith on the fruit; a zester will cut "ribbons" of zest.

CHOPPING BOARD

It's worth keeping a separate board just for use in cocktails. Cocktail flavours can be subtle and it's best if they are not attacked by a slice of orange cut on an onion-infused chopping board.

CITRUS JUICER/SQUEEZER

You can juice a lemon or lime by hand but a cocktail juicer will make it faster, easier and will extract far more juice.

ICE BUCKET AND ICE TONGS

Somewhat retro, but an insulated ice bucket is useful. We like to use a big rigid coolbox to hold ice. We jam a perforated stainless steel tray in the bottom to allow melt water to drip through, which keeps the ice in top condition.

TEA TOWEL AND ROLLING PIN

Wrap ice in a tea towel and bash with the rolling pin to make crushed ice.

BOTTLE OPENER AND CORKSCREW

Drinking essentials! Although you can make most cocktails without them.

CREAM WHIPPER

Absolutely not essential, but if you're going for advanced techniques such as infusions and foams (see pages 136–138 and 142), you'll need a cream whipper.

↓ MIXING GLASS   ↓ ICE BUCKET

↑ PEELER

↑ POURER

↙ ROLLING PIN

SPIRIT MEASURES ↓

PARING KNIFE ↗

TEA TOWEL ↘

↑ CITRUS JUICER

↙ ICE TONGS

↙ HAWTHORN STRAINER

↙ KITCHEN KNIFE

↓ CREAM WHIPPER

↓ ABSINTHE SPOON

↙ CORKSCREW

COBBLER SHAKER ↘

↓ BOTTLE OPENER

↑ JULEP STRAINER

↑ MUDDLER

CLASSICS

GIN COCKTAILS

Gin is a good spirit with which to start exploring cocktails. It is not the sort of thing that is generally drunk neat – it's too herby, too raw and just feels a bit wrong. But when smoothed with other ingredients it's a magical spirit. It's versatile and lends a satisfying clean flavour to a cocktail. Some people seem to believe that the Martini was invented so that gin could shamelessly be drunk neat, but a little vermouth and a lot of ice totally transforms gin; it's this transformation that is what cocktails are all about.

The simplest way to think of gin is as neutral alcohol (like vodka) that has been flavoured with herbs and spices. The gin distillation process is straightforward: a neutral grain spirit is redistilled with botanicals such as juniper, orange peel and coriander. Sometimes the botanicals are left to infuse in the spirit before distillation, and sometimes the botanicals don't go into the still but are placed in a basket above the still and the vapours passed through them. Hendrick's makes its distinctively flavoured gin by combining the distillates from a mixture of the two methods.

MARTINI

We've explored some Martini myths on pages 22–24.

4 PARTS GIN

1 PART DRY VERMOUTH

Add gin and vermouth to a mixing glass, cover with ice and stir well – about
30 seconds. Strain into a martini glass and garnish with a twist of lemon peel.
Larger quantities can be made in a jug.

GIN & TONIC

The delicious Hendrick's gin has been drunk in volume at many a Bompas & Parr
event. Making a Hendrick's and tonic couldn't be simpler.

1 PART HENDRICK'S GIN

3 PARTS INDIAN TONIC WATER

Fill a highball glass with ice. Pour the gin over and top up with the tonic water.
Garnish with a long slice of cucumber to complement the cucumber in the gin.
Alternatively, make a Gin Buck by swapping the tonic water for ginger ale.

WHISK(E)Y COCKTAILS

Whiskey (spelt whisky if you're talking about Scotch) is where you end up after a lifetime of drinking. It's a drink for heroes and some of the most glorious mixed drinks are whiskey based. All whiskies are made from distilled grain brews.

Scottish whisky (Scotch) and Irish whiskey are traditionally based on barley, although many include other grains – mixed grain whiskies tend to have a more neutral flavour. Nonetheless, Scotch whisky is generally sipped (perhaps with a little water) while American whiskies are more commonly used in mixed drinks. This is partly because in the golden age when cocktails were being developed, the old world whiskies wouldn't have been available to the mixed drinks pioneers.

Rye whiskey is the original spirit for cocktailing and is made mainly from rye (of course). It's slightly harsh on the palate but this is an advantage in

mixed drinks as it makes its character felt. Although rye went out of fashion for making cocktails it's now making a comeback and is the connoisseur's choice for a good Manhattan.

Bourbon is made from corn (maize) and is normally much sweeter than rye. When making a cocktail with bourbon, less sugar is needed; the bourbon will carry the day.

A Scotsman would be horrified if he caught you using Scotch to make a cocktail. That said, there are some fine and respectable cocktails, such as the Rob Roy, that call for the more husky character of Scotch whiskies to make them shine. Experiment by putting Scotch and Irish whiskies into mixed drinks and see if you can balance them out. Just don't let freaky drinks nationalists catch you doing it.

MANHATTAN

The Manhattan is a whiskey-based Martini. You can serve it either in a martini glass or with cubes of ice in an old-fashioned glass. The usual sweet, dry and perfect vermouth business applies (see page 22). Traditionalists always use rye to make a Manhattan. Being British, we like making Rob Roys – replace the whiskey with Scotch and garnish with a cherry.

2 PARTS RYE OR BOURBON WHISKEY
1 PART SWEET RED VERMOUTH
2 DASHES ANGOSTURA BITTERS

Stir the ingredients with ice in a mixing glass. Strain into a chilled cocktail glass. Garnish with a cherry or a twist of lemon peel.

PLUM SOUR

This is Harry's take on the whiskey sour; it came about because we've always got stewed plums and some sort of whisky in the studio. Stewing plums are the first stage of making a plum and red wine jelly, so when we're doing some epic jelly-making there are inevitably some plums bubbling away in the kitchen. The plums add another dimension to the bourbon and give the cocktail a satisfying colour. To make the stewed plums especially for this recipe, cut up a few plums and cook gently with some sugar. Adding a stick of cinnamon or a star anise to the plums works well too. Don't worry about straining – it will all come out when you do the final strain of the cocktail.

3 PARTS BOURBON
½ PART LEMON JUICE
½ PART STEWED PLUMS
SUGAR SYRUP (SEE PAGE 15) TO TASTE

Put the first three ingredients into an ice-filled shaker. Check for sweetness and add sugar syrup to taste. Shake hard and then strain into an ice-filled tumbler.

MINT JULEP

Traditionally this was served in a pewter or silver julep cup.

2 SPRIGS OF MINT
1 PART SUGAR SYRUP (SEE PAGE 15)
4 PARTS BOURBON

In either a highball glass or silver julep cup, muddle 1 sprig of mint with the sugar syrup. Fill the glass with crushed ice, add the bourbon and stir. Garnish with a sprig of mint.

WHISKEY SOUR

You need to shake a whiskey sour hard to get a decent foam on it: 30 seconds is about right. If you want foam that'll last until the end of your drink add a couple of teaspoons of egg white. When adding egg white to a cocktail we like to shake it without ice for a few seconds to get everything thoroughly mixed and then add the ice and continue on our way.

2 PARTS BOURBON
1 PART LEMON JUICE
1 PART SUGAR SYRUP (SEE PAGE 15)

Add all the ingredients to an ice-filled shaker. Shake really, really hard and then strain into an ice-filled tumbler.

OLD FASHIONED

The Old Fashioned is the original way of making rough booze more palatable by adding sugar and bitters. The traditional method is to wet a sugar cube with bitters and a little water and stir until it dissolves. This can be a bit of a bore — sugar syrup is much easier and gives a better result. For a more luxurious Old Fashioned, muddle a couple of orange slices and cherries in the bottom of a mixing glass with the sugar; add the whiskey and ice; stir; strain; and add a splash of soda to finish.

1 GLASS BOURBON
1 TSP SUGAR SYRUP (SEE PAGE 15)
3 DASHES ANGOSTURA BITTERS

Add everything to a low tumbler. Fill the glass with a couple of large ice cubes and stir for 10 seconds.

RUM COCKTAILS

Rum is a spirit of romance. It has a bit of a cocksure swagger, a shady past of slavery and piracy and is now receiving attention from spirit-sipping connoisseurs, historic cocktail scholars and third-wave tikiists. We love tiki. It is bawdy and brilliant. All those Samoan war clubs, bamboo, and broken bits of boat strapped to the ceiling.

Rum is distilled from sugar cane juice and molasses, the treacly waste product of crystal sugar manufacture. Dark rich rums are aged in wooden barrels; golden rums undergo less aging; clear, light rums may be unaged (rather fierce) or aged to smooth out the flavours, then filtered to remove the colour and hangover-inducing impurities.

Former French colony Martinique produces a rum called *rhum agricole*. As this is made from raw sugar cane juice and no molasses (like the Brazilian version cachaça) it is lighter and more vegetal, and delivers bewilderingly savage hangovers.

Don't be afraid to go tropical on the ingredients you put with your rum. It's invariably from an island paradise so it's OK to splash in coconut juice, spicy ginger brews, puréed mango — and garnish with a leafy pineapple top.

Many rum cocktail recipes call for a raft of different rums: white, golden and aged rums from exotic places like Jamaica, Cuba and Barbados. Don't be daunted. Mixing together a few different styles of rum can make for a far more complex drink, but if you don't have a drinks cabinet heaving with rare and unusual distillates, crack ahead with what you've got.

VODKA COCKTAILS

If you go to a super-trendy bar in Europe or America and ask for a vodka-based cocktail you'll be sneered at. It's the quickest way to show you are not part of the drinks cognoscenti. The better the vodka, the less flavour it has, so barmen who care about what their drinks taste like won't use it. Vodka buzzwords like "triple filtered" and "purity" equate to ripping out all the particles that give it an interesting taste. The spirit is reduced to fluid that will get you bent and cause the least flavour interference with whatever sugary fruit juice you have in your glass. Vodka manufacturers are fighting back with spirits made from gourmet potatoes from a single field but the damage is done. Among mixologists vodka isn't cool.

You're in for an even more haughty look if you want a flavoured vodka. There's been an explosion in the number of flavoured vodkas in the past decade: there are now 500 brands offering a bewildering array of flavours (blueberry, bubble gum, manuka honey, black cherry, cucumber, kaffir lime, hazelnut, Nordic berry). Who needs this rot? Especially as you can make your own pretty easily if you ever wanted to (see Infusions, pages 136–139).

But although vodka is thought lame by cocktail geeks it is the world's best-selling spirit, selling over half a billion cases per year. The haters are a bit like those indie kids who stop liking a band once they become popular.

Maybe there's a way to rehabilitate vodka while keeping sales high. We suggest looking east to mysterious Russia. You may think of yourself as an experienced vodka drinker who has mastered everything from vodka jelly to sophisticated Vesper martinis. To the average Russian your experience is nothing. They drink vodka with a steely determination and seriousness that has seen national male life expectancy down to 59.54 years, right above Ghana. This sounds grim but Russian vodka rituals have charm. They involve epic bouts of toasting, eating little snacks and then toasting again. Never drink before the toast, always drain your glass, remove empty bottles from the table and keep eating the little snacks and you'll be OK. Feel transported to a land of throbbing discothèques, casual sex and theremins. Far cooler than any precious bar that won't serve vodka.

TEQUILA FIZZ

3 PARTS TEQUILA
½ PART LEMON JUICE
½ PART LIME JUICE
1 TBSP SUGAR SYRUP (SEE PAGE 15)
½ EGG WHITE

Pour all ingredients into a cocktail shaker. Shake without ice for a few seconds.
Add ice, shake and pour into a highball glass. Garnish with a slice of lime.

MARGARITA

There's no point in denying this is an absolutely delicious drink. Even if it's a kind
of dudes' version of a tequila slammer with all the components stuck into the glass.

2 PARTS TEQUILA
1 PART COINTREAU
1 PART LIME JUICE

Start by rimming a chilled martini glass with salt. Rub a slice of lime around
the outside rim and carefully roll the edge through a plate of coarse sea salt. To
make the cocktail, shake the ingredients with ice and strain into the glass.

TEQUILA SUNRISE

Naff but pretty. It's normally made in a highball glass but use a martini glass if you like.

1 PART TEQUILA
3 PARTS ORANGE JUICE
1 TSP GRENADINE

Shake the tequila and orange juice with plenty of ice and strain into a highball glass. Pour in the grenadine and watch the sunrise. Garnish with a tropical jungle of orange wheels, cherries and little cocktail swords.

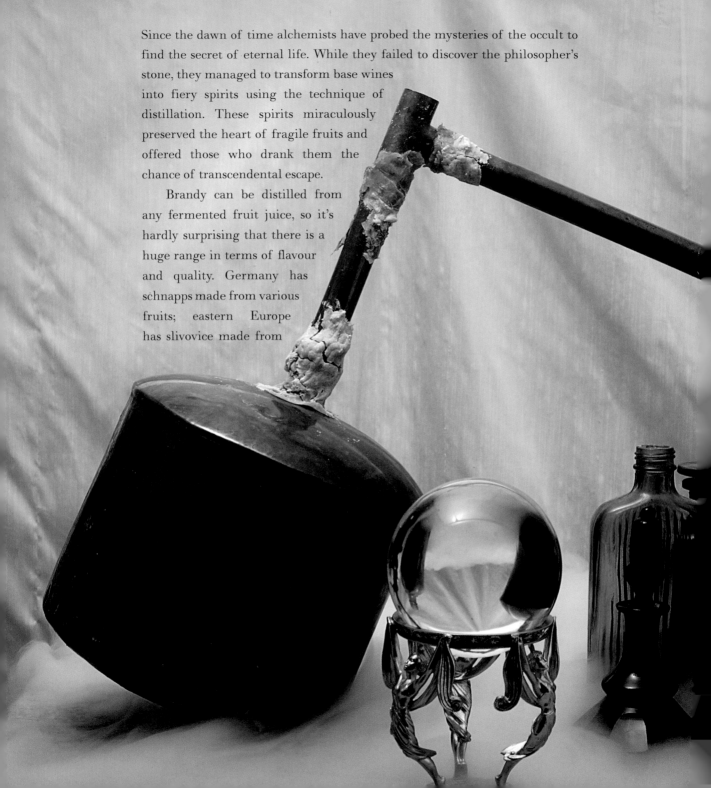

BRANDY COCKTAILS

Since the dawn of time alchemists have probed the mysteries of the occult to find the secret of eternal life. While they failed to discover the philosopher's stone, they managed to transform base wines into fiery spirits using the technique of distillation. These spirits miraculously preserved the heart of fragile fruits and offered those who drank them the chance of transcendental escape.

Brandy can be distilled from any fermented fruit juice, so it's hardly surprising that there is a huge range in terms of flavour and quality. Germany has schnapps made from various fruits; eastern Europe has slivovice made from plums. However, most cocktails that include brandy are looking for grape- or apple-based distillates. Apple-based brandies are wonderful in mixed drinks (see Poor Man's Champagne Cocktail, page 82). Calvados comes from Normandy and some decent apple brandies are now being made in the US.

Cognac is distilled from wine made in a specific region of South West France. It comes in various grades: look for the letters near the brand name. VS (Very Special) is aged in wood for at least two years and is not that special: one for the winos! VSOP (Very Superior Old Pale) is aged in wood for at least four years and is a good choice for making cocktails. Finally, there is XO (Extra Old): for sipping rather than mixing.

France also produces armagnac, which uses wine from the Gascony region; it is similarly graded but a little more savage than cognac.

Cognac was used in many early cocktails and mixed drinks and has a long history as a party pleaser. Sadly, it fell into neglect when the phylloxera blight hammered French wine production in the late 19th century. Now cognac is back in favour, as it can bring a richness and glowing depth to a cocktail.

SIDE CAR

The sidecar is really just a brandy sour in which the sugar syrup is replaced by orange liqueur. We've suggested a ratio that we like, but you could go for equal parts (the most usual way) or hit the cognac hard, depending on your mood (or whether it's decent brandy). It's worth sugaring the rim of the glass first, as the added sweetness really helps the flavours come together.

2 PARTS COGNAC

1 PART ORANGE LIQUEUR (COINTREAU OR GRAND MARNIER)

1 PART LEMON JUICE

1 TSP SUGAR SYRUP (SEE PAGE 15)

Shake all the ingredients with ice. Strain into a sugar-rimmed cocktail glass. Garnish with orange peel.

KINGSLEY AMIS'S MILK PUNCH

As well as writing raunchy books, Kingsley Amis was a smashing if cantankerous drinks writer. Here's his version of a party drink that's good for winter. He said the only difficult part is remembering to freeze milk in ice cube trays the day before. Sam also likes this with gin, but it's pretty hardcore. For a tamer version try the White Cargo on page 145.

1 PART BRANDY

1 PART BOURBON WHISKEY

1 PART SUGAR SYRUP (SEE PAGE 15)

4 PARTS MILK

FROZEN MILK CUBES

NUTMEG

Put milk instead of water in some ice cube trays the day before, so you get frozen milk cubes.

Mix the brandy, bourbon, sugar syrup and milk in a jug. Pour into glasses and drop in the frozen milk cubes. Dust with grated nutmeg and serve.

SAZERAC

The Sazerac, an old-fashioned style of cocktail, has always been New Orleans' cocktail of choice. Originally made with the French cognac Sazerac de Forge et Fils, American rye whiskey took its place when cognac became hard to get after phylloxera struck French vineyards in the 1880s. If you want to create a traditional American Sazerac, you should use Sazerac Rye Whiskey, Peychaud's Bitters (invented in New Orleans) and Herbsaint pastis instead of absinthe.

SPLASH ABSINTHE

1 GLASS COGNAC

1 TSP SUGAR SYRUP (SEE PAGE 15)

3 DASHES ANGOSTURA BITTERS

Splash the absinthe into a glass, swirl it and then pour it out. This will give a good hit of absinthe on the nose, but it won't overpower the cognac. Place in the freezer to chill down. Combine the remaining ingredients in a mixing glass filled with ice and stir well. Strain into the absinthe-coated glass.

CHAMPAGNE COCKTAILS

"Ask your guests what they would like to drink. If they say that they do not mind it means they want Champagne." SAVOY COCKTAIL BOOK

Champagne is mostly overrated and always overpriced. The carbon dioxide from the bubbles makes your breath smell like feet but a bottle does make life fun and canny cocktail skills can result in a decent drink. Grimod de La Reynière (1758–1837), the first proper food critic and prodigious gourmand, explains the appeal of champagne:

> *"Champagne is certainly not the best wine, but it is the wine the ladies prefer. Sacrifices have to be made to their tastes in the hope that we will be favoured by some pleasant prattle and the blithe bursts of a delicate erotic gaity. In general the arrival of champagne is the cue for a gentle liberty to begin to reassert its right."*

The beauty of champagne lies in the expense, the ritual and fireworks of opening a bottle and the fact that the carbonated beverages get your guests

intoxicated quicker. A team from the University of Surrey gave subjects equal amounts of sparkling and flat champagne containing the same levels of alcohol. Five minutes after downing the drink, the group who'd had sparkling champagne had 54 milligrams of alcohol in their blood, while those on the flat stuff had only 39 milligrams. The bubbles carry alcohol into the lungs so it can go straight into the bloodstream, bypassing the liver. Party on!

Champagne and champagne cocktails are generally acceptable with almost anything and at any time of the day. They are also simple to make. The aim of most champagne cocktails is to make champagne taste better and be far more potent.

OUR FAVOURITES

GETTING DRUNK ON THE CHEAP

Alcohol is expensive. Unless you distill your own on the sly you'll be at the mercy of high taxes and big brands. One option is to buy the cheapest booze going, and with a little magic, turn it into something special. That is a big part of what cocktails are about. But you can push it much harder if you think outside of the glass.

The key is the environment that you drink in. Drinkers at the American Bar at the Savoy hotel in London are happy to drop £14 on one cocktail. The weight of history, the fancy white uniforms and the astounding bar make the price acceptable, even though a penny-pinching boozer could use that same £14 to go on a three-day bender, as long as they stuck to park-bench beverages like super-strength canned cider. But if you drink in a space that looks magical, with proper service, the experience will be awesome.

We use this principle when designing food installations. Although we pay great attention to the food and drink, that's only about 20 per cent of the work: the brute effort goes into building extraordinary dining and drinking environments, rigging the lighting, sourcing the tableware and making sure the service is excellent.

When we produced The Complete History of Food event in July 2010 – an edible epic so magnificent that it spanned 730 years – the challenge was to turn a Mayfair house into a dining adventure. We wanted guests to feel that they were eating their way through history as they moved between the spaces. We used four design crews to build environments that evoked different eras, including a flooded dining room with live eels in the water, a giant inflatable stomach and a working bar created from living plants

POOR MAN'S CHAMPAGNE COCKTAIL

1 SUGAR CUBE
ANGOSTURA BITTERS
1 TBSP CALVADOS
CIDER, WELL CHILLED

Place the sugar cube in a champagne flute, soak it with bitters, add the calvados and top up with chilled cider. Garnish with a slice of apple.

ABSINTHE

There is a great deal of mystique around absinthe, the powerful and highly alcoholic anise-flavoured spirit that was banned for most of the 20th century in the US and much of Europe. It was hugely popular among French artists and writers such as Baudelaire and Toulouse-Lautrec in the mid- to late-19th century, but the evil "green fairy" was also blamed for many of society's ills. In 1905 a Swiss alcoholic called Jean Lanfray murdered his family while drunk on absinthe. The worldwide hysteria surrounding absinthe's purported vicious and hallucinogenic qualities led to it being banned. It turns out that while the spirit does contain hallucinogenic thujone it is not at a level that would have any significant results. So absinthe is back in bars, which is good news.

Absinthe gets its flavour primarily from anise, fennel and wormwood, along with other herbs. It plays an important supporting role in cocktails, such as the Sazerac, and we sometimes use a thimbleful of absinthe in punches such as Black Gin Punch (see page 108) to bring them to life. The flavours in absinthe are so full-on that you only need a tiny bit to make a cocktail shine: a dash, a glass rinsed with the spirit or even a spritz of absinthe from a perfume bottle across the top of the drink to finish it. Have a play next time you are making a drink.

The brilliant thing about absinthe is the paraphernalia that goes with. There's a wealth of excellent vintage kit, such as absinthe fountains – which drip iced water slowly into six glasses of absinthe – and absinthe spoons. Sam is obsessed by the lurid green uranium glass that was produced to showcase the colours of absinthe. These glasses glow eerily under a UV light, as they were made with sands containing depleted uranium. They are super-rare, so if you see one snatch it up.

If you want to drink absinthe on its own there are a couple of ways to do it. Either way will involve sugaring it and adding water to make it palatable:

- The Bohemian method is to pour a glass of absinthe, take a teaspoonful of granulated sugar and dip the tip in the glass so absinthe soaks into the sugar. When the sugar is sodden, light it and watch it burn. As soon as all the sugar has melted, tip the flaming concoction into the glass of absinthe at the same time as pouring in a glassful of water (the same size glass as for the absinthe), extinguishing the flame. This is always messy but can be fun.
- The Parisian method (more traditional) is to sit a sugar cube on a perforated spoon over a glass of absinthe and slowly drip ice-cold water through the sugar cube. Marvel as the oils in the absinthe louche from clear to a cloudy opacity as the water drips into the glass. Continue until the booze/sugar/water balance suits your palate.

ETHER COCKTAIL

We set out to conquer ether after Sam read an oblique reference to a champagne and diethyl ether cocktail causing chaos in late 19th-century London. It sounded worth investigating and thrillingly dangerous. We first experimented with ether at a special breakfast event and we have gone on to use ether at other events.

Before becoming the world's most widely used anaesthetic ether was a popular recreational drug used by society scientists and Northern Irish crofters alike. A *New York Times* article of 1880 describes its use:

> *Ether was often used by young people in many places in the United States. They had what they called "ether frolics" in which they inhaled ether till they became merry, or in some other way absurdly excited, or, in some cases, completely insensible.*

Ether is extremely volatile. It is highly flammable and the vapours are dense. Be warned it is liable to explode if it is in the proximity of open flames.

Ether can have some side effects including respiratory irritation and cause headaches but generally the effects are similar to those of booze, albeit much more short-lived! Ether drinkers can be drunk and sober five or six times in a single day.

One way to take ether is by inhaling from an ether-soaked rag (gag'n'rag), just like in Hunter S. Thompson's *Fear and Loathing in Las Vegas*. The 19th-century Irish way was to drink a glass of water, take one drop of ether while holding your nose and then slam down another glass of water. The ether is so volatile you need the water to wash it down otherwise it will evaporate. The problem with both these is the ether smell is utterly overwhelming and hard to love on its own.

Here's the best way to drink ether. Dropping the ether on the strawberry prevents it from evaporating immediately and the sharp hospital tang of the ether is strangely complemented by the strawberries and champagne.

Serves 6

8ML/¼FL OZ DIETHYL ETHER (SEE PAGE 156)

6 STRAWBERRIES

1 BOTTLE CHAMPAGNE

Place two drops of diethyl ether on a strawberry. Put the strawberry in a champagne flute and fill with chilled champagne.

A word of warning – the ether is dangerously flammable

OLD & OBSCURE

CHILDREN & ALCOHOL

Think of underage drinking and you'll probably imagine hooded youths on a park bench or teenage girls throwing up into their handbags after a night out, yet the historical relationship between children and alcohol is one more concerned with custom and rites of passage than who can drink the most. Even in recent times it has been customary to rub whisky into a baby's gums while it's teething, or for older children to take whisky and lemon juice when they're ill.

Alcohol as a rite of passage, particularly as a bond between father and son, has a long tradition. Silver tankards were popular as christening presents from the 17th century until relatively recently. By the late-19th century the connection between alcohol and the masculine family bond had matured into gifts of wine, predominantly port, on birthdays and christenings.

Birthdays always offer opportunities for drinking and Mrs Beeton perfected an alcoholic punch for children's parties. This punch, known as Negus, has an interesting history: created by Colonel Francis Negus in the early 18th century, it began as an elegant and refined concoction, but as with the once aristocratic jelly it soon became a children's party staple.

NEGUS

From Mrs Beeton's Book of Household Management, *originally published in 1861.*
"As this beverage is more usually drunk at children's parties than at any other, the wine need not be very old or expensive… Negus may also be made of sherry, or a sweet white wine, but is more usually made of port than of any other beverage."

Serves 9 or 10 children

125G/4OZ SUGAR
JUICE AND GRATED ZEST OF 1 LEMON
½ GRATED NUTMEG
1 LITRE/1¾ PINTS BOILING WATER
500ML/18FL OZ PORT WINE

Put the sugar, lemon zest and nutmeg into a large heatproof jug. Pour the boiling water over and stir until the sugar has dissolved. Add the strained juice of the lemon and the port. Allow to cool a little before serving.

HOT MILK POSSET

The traditional nanny's remedy for insomniac children (and frail heroines) looks well designed to put a person to sleep.

Serves 6

500ML/18FL OZ MILK

DASH ALMOND ESSENCE

½ TSP GRATED LEMON ZEST

50G/1¾OZ CASTER SUGAR

1 EGG WHITE, BEATEN

60ML/2FL OZ RUM

125ML/4FL OZ BRANDY

Warm the milk with the almond essence, lemon zest and sugar. Take off the heat and whisk in the egg white until the drink is frothy. Add the rum and brandy and serve hot. Sweet dreams.

CAPTAIN FRASER

Sam writes: Captain Fraser was my great-grandfather. He is my hero. I've had his picture hanging on my wall my entire life alongside a picture of his ship, SS *Hirano Maru*, decked out in spectacular camouflage.

The story of Captain Fraser's life and untimely death has always given me goosebumps. It is romantic, noble, and has been an inspiration and goad to hard work and adventure.

The *Hirano Maru* was a Japanese merchant navy liner, weighing a mighty 7,935 tons. On 1 October 1918 she left Liverpool on her homeward voyage, captained by Hector Fraser. The First World War was coming to an end and an armistice was five weeks away; the weather was brutal. On 4 October at 5.15am, when 60 miles (96 kilometres) from the Irish coast, the *Hirano Maru* was hit in the hold by a torpedo from a German submarine. Minutes later a second torpedo hit the middle of the boiler room. Within seven minutes the ship nose-dived and went straight to the bottom.

Passengers and crew leapt into the sea but by the time an American torpedo-destroyer came to the rescue in response to the SOS many people were so overcome by cold that for the most part they were unable to take hold of the ropes thrown to them; 292 lives were lost; only 28 survived. Captain Fraser was last seen on the bridge of the *Hirano Maru* going down with the ship.

CAPTAIN FRASER'S GROG

Serves 2

4 PARTS DARK RUM (PUSSER'S NAVY RUM IS BEST)

4 PARTS HOT WATER

1 PART LIME JUICE

1 PART BROWN SUGAR SYRUP (SEE PAGE 15)

Mix all the ingredients in a heatproof measuring jug and pour into tumblers or mugs. Garnish with a slice of orange and a cinnamon stick or with mint as here.

Alexis Soyer was the Jamie Oliver of his day. He revolutionized the modern kitchen (championing gas cookery) while working at the Reform Club in London, invented a mobile soup kitchen to feed victims of the Irish Potato Famine and saved troops from malnutrition in the Crimean War, working alongside Florence Nightingale. He also wrote best-selling books, manipulated the media and launched products such as Soyer's Nectar, a blue lemonade sold as a health drink.

Soyer was a flamboyant self-publicist who adopted the zig-zag as his signature glyph. All his clothes were cut on the bias, dishes were topped with zig-zag attelets and pastries also bore the pattern.

His greatest adventure came during London's Great Exhibition of 1851. Soyer, the leading celebrity chef, was offered exclusive rights to the catering for the Crystal Palace built in Hyde Park. He refused, because influence from the temperance movement meant that alcohol was not allowed to be served with meals. Soyer didn't think you could have a civilized meal without booze. Soyer chose instead to create his own Great Exhibition of food at Gore House, adjacent to Hyde Park. He ambitiously called it Soyer's Universal Symposium of all Nations and it was effectively a food and drink theme park. It included an ice cave with stalactites of real ice that had to be shipped in daily (at the time there was no refrigeration) and stuffed snow foxes, a medieval banqueting hall, a weather chamber where arcs of electricity fizzed across the ceiling imitating sheet lightning, and a grotto you had to plunge through a waterfall to reach. Entrance to the grotto was free but you'd get wet unless you hired one of Soyer's umbrellas.

The Symposium, though spectacular, was hugely overambitious and ended amid massive financial complications. It did, however, bring mixed drinks and cocktails to the attention of London society. One of the few lucrative elements was the Washington Bar attached to the Symposium. The blades of society could choose from over 40 beverages, which included some of Soyer's own invention, like this Soyer au Champagne.

1 TBSP VANILLA ICE CREAM

1 PART MARASCHINO LIQUEUR (WE USE LUXARDO)

1 PART ORANGE CURAÇAO

1 PART BRANDY

CHAMPAGNE

Build the first four ingredients in a champagne flute and fill with champagne.
Garnish with an orange slice and a cherry. Think of it as a champagne float.

Punches
& Party drinks

ARCHITECTURAL PUNCH BOWL

Punches pre-date cocktails by a couple of hundred years. First documented in 1632, they dominated the mixed drink scene at a time when friends who could afford expensive alcohol could also afford to sit down and spend several hours drinking and talking.

The word "punch" is thought to be derived from the Hindi *panch* (meaning five) and the drink was originally made with five ingredients: alcohol (rum or brandy), sugar, lemon, water and tea or spices. This might sound quite a basic mixture, but in the early 17th century this punch would be drawing together exotic and expensive ingredients from all corners of the known world.

England, at the centre of a maritime trading empire, led the world in punch-making and a British admiral, stationed in Alicante in 1694, is responsible for possibly the most extraordinary mixed drink in history — it's number two in our top ten drinking stories (see page 10). We learnt about Admiral Edward Russell's punch from an alcohol academic and after hearing the story there was no going back.

We were so inspired by the story that we had to bring it to London. A UK government-funded research project with the UCL Bartlett School of Architecture established that it would be possible to overcome the food hygiene and structural challenges inherent in building the world's largest punch bowl.

So with Courvoisier's support we teamed up with engineers Arup and the food safety team at London South Bank University to flood a building with booze. For our greatest alcohol adventure to date we created the Architectural Punch Bowl, which allowed people to boat across a four-tonne punch before having a glass. The recipe we used was based on the Emperor's Shrub (see next page).

Hotshot mixologist Joe McCanta came up with this winning recipe. The genius of Joe's recipe is that it lasts for ages — it is so acidic and alcoholic and sugary that bacteria don't stand a chance — so it was really suitable for a punch that had to be out for four days.

Here's what Joe says about shrubs: "Shrubs are a mix of fresh berries, sugar and vinegar that serve as a cordial to be mixed with any type of alcohol, but most often brandy and rum, which were the most readily available spirits in 17th- and 18th-century England. Ice wasn't an important ingredient in drinks until the early 1800s, and the success of the shrub was partly due to the fact that it provided a thirst-quenching tang and offered an amazing balance of sweet and tart without needing to be chilled. Shrubs are simple to make and a batch can last for months, even unrefrigerated — and best of all they grow brighter and more flavourful over time as the berries and spices seep into the delicious liquid."

FISH HOUSE PUNCH

The flavours of this punch are so muscly you can really gorge on it. The punch is an old American formula devised by gentleman's sporting club the Schuylkill Fishing Company. The club was founded in 1732 with "citizens" meeting every second Wednesday (from May to October) to cook, eat and drink together.

It was unusual in that the 25 citizens, 5 apprentices and their guests did all the work of gutting fish, roasting meat, mixing punch and washing up without recourse to servants. Democratic in comparison to other posh drinking, dining and debating clubs of the time, it was visited by two presidents, George Washington and Chester Arthur, who were likewise made to pitch in.

The punch was traditionally made in a bowl big enough to serve as the baptismal font for the members' children. If it's too alcoholic for your taste, dilute with chilled black tea.

Serves 20

400ML/14FL OZ SUGAR SYRUP (SEE PAGE 15)
400ML/14FL OZ COLD WATER
300ML/10FL OZ LEMON JUICE
500ML/18FL OZ RUM
1 BOTTLE (700ML) COGNAC
100ML/3½ FL OZ PEACH BRANDY

Stir the sugar syrup and water together in a large bowl. Add the lemon juice, rum, cognac and peach brandy. Cover the bowl and chill for at least 3 hours.

Put a 2-litre/3½ pint block of ice (which can be made by freezing a large bowl of water overnight) in a punch bowl and pour the punch over it. Garnish with lemon slices.

EGGNOG

Eggnog is a fine winter drink. It masterfully combines fat, sugar, salt and alcohol to give your body what it needs in cold weather. It stimulates neurons, cells that trigger the brain's reward system and release dopamine, a chemical that motivates our behaviour and makes us want to have more. Many of us have what's called a "bliss point", at which we get the greatest pleasure from sugar, fat or salt. Combined in the right way, these flavour "building blocks" can make a product indulgent and high in "hedonic value". Eggnog gets this pretty much spot on.

The drink polarizes people, because many can't stand the eggyness. They are missing out. This is a good drink (even if it is once a year).

Serves 24

12 LARGE EGGS, SEPARATED
200G/7OZ DARK BROWN SUGAR
DASH VANILLA ESSENCE
PINCH OF SALT
250ML/9FL OZ RUM
250ML/9FL OZ BRANDY
1 LITRE/1¾ PINTS FULL-FAT MILK
1 LITRE/1¾ PINTS DOUBLE CREAM
1 NUTMEG FOR GRATING

In a large mixing bowl, combine the yolks, sugar, vanilla and salt and beat to the consistency of cream before mixing in the rum and brandy.

Beat the egg whites to a stiff froth and beat them into the mixture, then stir in the milk and cream. Pour into small cups and garnish by grating the nutmeg over the top.

For extra finesse, add 100ml/3½fl oz Madeira as suggested by the pioneer of American cocktails, Jerry Thomas. You could use bourbon or even Scotch instead of the brandy and rum, though this will make more of a backwoods-style feral eggnog.

CURES

A punishing hangover is a firm disincentive to heavy drinking. Sadly, hangovers are still poorly understood from a medical perspective. Physically, hangovers are caused by general dehydration, acute ethanol (alcohol) withdrawal, hypoglycemia (not enough blood sugar) and by-products of alcoholic fermentation called congeners. Psychologically, there's the crippling shame in recalling (or not being able to recall) what you did the night before.

The best way to avoid hangovers is not to drink. If you *are* going to drink then make sure water goes in too. This is something to bear in mind for your guests: a glass of ice water on the side will certainly be appreciated the next day. There's a lot of balls about not mixing grape and grain or dark and light drinks. Don't worry too much about this. On a night when you've had half a bottle of red wine, crème de menthe, two Negronis and a little glass of aged rum, you've had a considerable amount to drink. Mixing drinks is beside the point.

One effective way of impeding the symptoms of a hangover is to ingest more alcohol. This will buy you time. The effects on your insides may at first be alarming but this will soon be replaced with a warm glow. You can use the extra hours to get in water and sugar, which will help soften the blow when the hammer falls.

FERNET BRANCA

Fernet Branca has a serious cult following in America. It tastes like Odin's breath fresh from the underworld and professional chefs and barmen use it as a bibulous Masonic handshake. If you are drinking shots of Fernet Branca you are in the know.

The great Fergus Henderson has a recipe for overindulgence he calls "A Miracle": two parts Fernet Branca with one part crème de menthe over ice.

Fernet is an Italian *amaro*, a bitter spirit held to have medicinal properties. The syrupy brown liquid contains a secret combination of herbs and spices with notes of myrrh, rhubarb, saffron, camomile and cardamom to kick you into shape. Hold on tight when you have your first shot. It's absolutely biblical and will horrify, exhilarate and inspire.

Drink Fernet Branca at room temperature or over ice, or use it instead of Angostura in cocktails like the Manhattan. Always have a bottle in your life and it'll rescue you from many a hangover.

HANKY PANKY

This Martini variation is a beast of a cocktail to knock back in the morning. It was created by the Savoy hotel's first head bartender, Ada Coleman, who reigned at the American Bar from its opening in 1898. Impressively, there have been only ten head bartenders in the entire history of the American Bar.

2 DASHES FERNET BRANCA

1 PART SWEET VERMOUTH

1 PART GIN

Stir in a mixing glass over ice and strain into a martini glass. Garnish with a large twist of orange peel. This is a great reviver.

TOBACCO ELIXIR

This will bring you back to life, but if you get addicted it may give you cancer. It's excellent to serve at the end of a punishing meal. We use Black Cavendish tobacco (see Suppliers, page 156); it has a vanilla note that complements the coffee.

3 PARTS BOURBON

1 PART TOBACCO SYRUP (SEE BELOW)

DASH OF STRONG ESPRESSO

For the tobacco syrup

125ML/4FL OZ WATER

125G/4OZ CASTER SUGAR

20G/¾OZ GOOD TOBACCO

First make the tobacco syrup. Bring the water to the boil, then remove from the heat and stir in the sugar and tobacco. Continue stirring until all the sugar has dissolved. Let the tobacco infuse for 10 minutes, then strain the syrup through a sieve to remove the leaves.

Combine the bourbon, tobacco syrup and espresso and decant into a medicine bottle. Serve on teaspoons at the end of a meal to make people feel better/send them over the edge.

TECHNIQUES

FLAMING

Setting fire to things is exciting – just ask any arsonist. Without burning down your house, there is still plenty of fun to be had with setting fire to alcohol. Burning booze has two effects. Firstly it adds character to a cocktail, as the heat creates new flavours; secondly, it just looks amazing.

In order to ignite alcohol it helps if the alcohol content is really high (over-proof rums and the like are great) and it's even better if you can heat up the liquid before torching it. If you are making a Sazerac it's fun to rinse the glass with absinthe and then ignite the absinthe with a match. It looks spectacular and you'll still get a good absinthe hit on the nose. To go all out with flames, you can get hold of a special atomizer that allows you to spray a fine mist of alcohol. When you hold a lighter in front of this it turns it into a flamethrower.

For a more subtle flaming experience you can set fire to the natural oils in orange and lemon peel. Flaming works best on large fresh oranges and lemons, as they have thicker skins; navel oranges work best of all. First step is to cut some oval-shaped "twists" from the fruit (see page 131). Take the twist and hold it over the glass, peel side down. Be careful not to squeeze it yet as this will release the oils. Take a lit match and hold it between the glass and the peel. Squeeze sharply and the oils will be released and propelled through the flame onto the surface of the drink.

A fun garnish for tiki punches is to create a flaming passion fruit boat to float across the surface of the drink. Cut a passion fruit in half and remove the pulp. Then heat up some overproof rum, fill the passion fruit shells and float on the surface of the drink. Then dim the lights and carefully ignite.

There's a trend for bars to serve their own infused spirits. These infusions, complex as they sound, are easy to make. The challenge lies in deciding what to infuse.

Alcohol is an excellent solvent, so given a bit of time will extract flavours from just about anything thrown into a bottle, from chewing gum to lavender. The method is to add your chosen ingredient to a bottle of booze and wait. Give the bottle an occasional shake. It takes on average a day for the flavour to be extracted. Then strain through coffee filter paper or a fine wire sieve into a jug and when all has dripped through pour back into the bottle.

You don't have to sacrifice a whole bottle of booze for your infusion. There are two options: either make smaller quantities, in a sealed container, or try the fast, fun "nitrogen cavitation" technique (see page 138).

MARTINI PROVENCALE

Here's a "Provençale" martini from the mighty Employees Only bar in Manhattan.

2½ PARTS LAVENDER-INFUSED GIN (SEE BELOW)
2½ PARTS VERMOUTH DE PROVENCE (SEE BELOW)
1 PART COINTREAU

First make the infusions. For the lavender-infused gin, place 1½ teaspoons dried lavender in a bottle of gin and leave for a day, shaking the bottle occasionally. For the vermouth, pour 180ml/6fl oz Noilly Prat into a small pan, add 2¼ teaspoons dried herbes de Provence and heat gently for a few minutes; leave to cool and then strain back into the bottle.

For each cocktail, measure the parts into a mixing glass, stir with ice and strain into a cocktail glass. Garnish with a twist of orange peel.

EGGS

Mixing with eggs has a profound effect on cocktails. If you add a whole egg white to a sour and give it a really good shake it makes a cocktail with a frothy head – like a badly poured pint of Guinness. Too much egg white is not a great thing, because it is fairly flavourless and it tends to just sit on top of the drink, lingering until your last gulp; the Pisco Sour (below) is one of the few cocktails that has a really thick foam. A couple of teaspoons of egg white per cocktail gives a better result, as even a brief shake will give you a head that combines with the rest of the drink. This technique works well with a whiskey sour.

Egg yolks, when shaken into drinks, help to smooth all the other ingredients together and create a cocktail with a velvety texture. The ultimate egg-based drink is the Eggnog, a recipe for which is to be found on page 108.

Adding any amount of whole egg to a cocktail will give a velvety, slightly aerated texture. The trick with using eggs is to give the mixture a shake first without adding ice: this helps the egg white to foam and emulsify. Then open up the shaker, add ice and continue on your way.

It goes without saying that when using eggs make sure that they are fresh and of the highest quality. Although we reckon that the alcohol and acidity in a cocktail is not bacteria friendly, you don't want to be known as the person who got knocked off by a fancy drink.

PISCO SOUR

The Pisco Sour is an excellent egg-based cocktail made with pisco, a clear grape brandy made in Chile and Peru.

2 PARTS PISCO

1 PART LIME JUICE

1 PART SUGAR SYRUP (SEE PAGE 15)

1 EGG WHITE

2 DASHES BITTERS

Put all the ingredients, except the bitters, into a shaker. Remove the spring from a hawthorn strainer (see page 27) and shake all the ingredients together with the spring. The spring helps to create a firm foam. Remove the spring, top the shaker up with ice cubes, shake again, then strain into a martini or coupe glass. Sprinkle the bitters on to the foam.

FOAMS

Foams can be made by adding egg white to a cocktail and shaking it vigorously. But almost as soon as it's poured, the heavier ingredients fall out of suspension and back into the cocktail below. So the foam is mainly egg white and lacking in flavour – it's certainly not a foamed version of the cocktail.

However, if you use a cream whipper to do the shaking for you, all the flavours get nicely amalgamated. You can make a cocktail that has the clarity and smoothness of a stirred drink, topped with the contrasting velvety texture of a foam.

If you want to make foam-topped drinks for a party, then the whipper method is the way to go. You can stir big quantities of drinks in a jug and then top with ready-made foam. Our friend Dave Hart, from the Institute of Food Research, likes to turn up to parties with a charged whipper full of Pimm's foam ready to make any drink that bit more fun.

The general key to success with making a flavoured foam is to include an acidic/sour component (such as lemon juice), a sweetening agent (such as sugar syrup) and some water. The sugar and the acid help to stabilize the foam. The water keeps the foam light. It's a good idea to chill the charged canister for an hour in the fridge or leave it on ice. This further stabilizes the foam and makes it last for much longer once put into the glass. You can prepare a foam well in advance; once charged, the nitrous oxide (N2O, in the whipper charger) acts to deter bacterial growth.

Here are the amounts we'd normally use in a 1-litre cream whipper:

4 EGG WHITES
100ML/3½ FL OZ SUGAR SYRUP (SEE PAGE 15)
50ML//1¾ FL OZ LEMON OR LIME JUICE
100ML/3½ FL OZ WATER

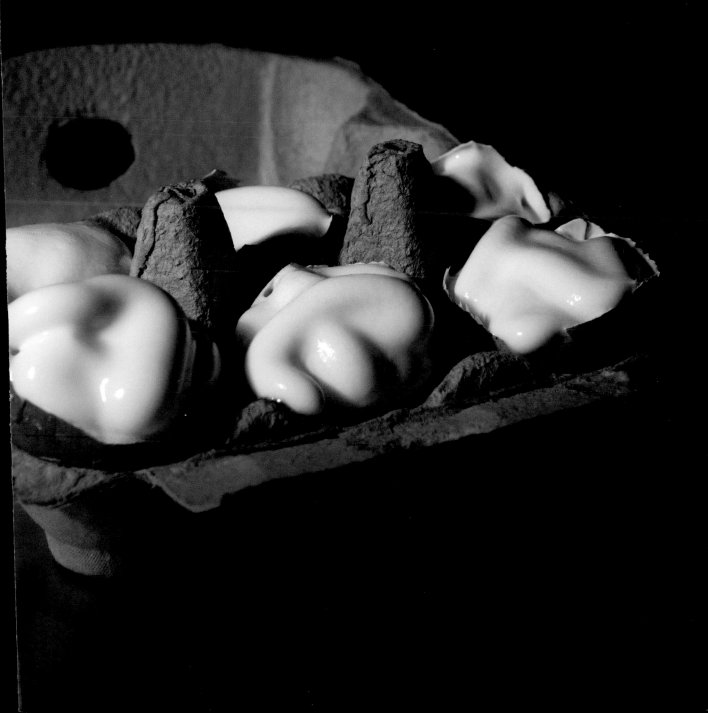

GOLDEN SYRUP OLD FASHIONED

You'll need a cream whipper to make this old-school cocktail with a glittering foam on top.

Serves 4

280ML/9½FL OZ SCOTCH WHISKY

1½ TSP ANGOSTURA BITTERS

2 TSP SUGAR SYRUP (SEE PAGE 15)

For the foam

40ML/1½FL OZ WATER

20G/¾OZ GOLDEN SYRUP

1 EGG WHITE

15ML/½FL OZ LEMON JUICE

1 TSP GOLD POWDER (OPTIONAL, SEE SUPPLIERS, PAGE 156)

First make the foam. Heat the water in a small pan, add the golden syrup and stir until the syrup is thoroughly dissolved. Leave to cool. Add the syrup mixture to a cream whipper and add the egg whites, lemon juice and gold powder. Give it a little shake and charge the whipper with N2O. Place in the fridge for at least 1 hour.

When ready to serve, stir the Scotch, bitters and sugar syrup with ice in a mixing glass. Carefully squirt the foam into four cocktail glasses, filling them about half full. Strain the cocktail into the glasses. The gold foam will float to the surface.

ICE CREAM

Ice cream added to cocktails is genius. The ice cream is sweet, so you don't need to add sugar; it's freezing cold, so you don't need ice; and it's damn tasty. Instant boozy milkshake.

WHITE CARGO

One of our favourite ice cream cocktails is the White Cargo; it's a really straight-forward recipe and everyone loves it. We like to serve it with a bucket of Quail Cottage (see recipe, page 153).

Serves 20
2 LITRES/3½ PINTS VANILLA ICE CREAM
1 BOTTLE HENDRICK'S GIN
180ML/6FL OZ MARASCHINO LIQUEUR (WE USE LUXARDO)
NUTMEG

Put all the ingredients (except the nutmeg) into a punch bowl. Wait until the ice cream has mostly melted, stir and then top with grated nutmeg. Serve in teacups.

This can also be made in smaller quantities. Either shake the ingredients together (without ice) or use a blender as if making a milkshake.

BAR SNACKS

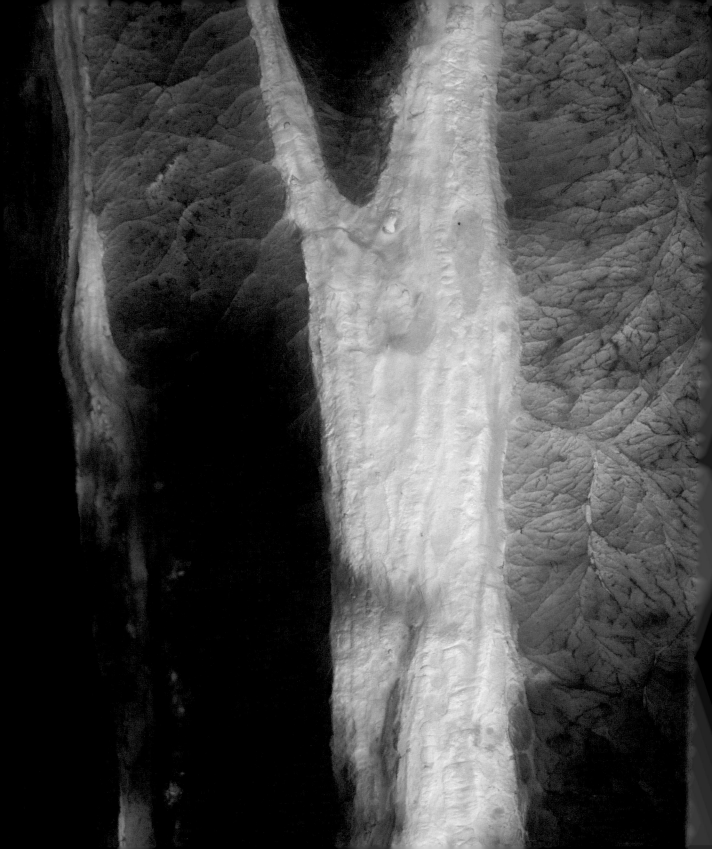

BACON FRAZZLES

Frazzles "crispy bacon flavour corn snacks" deliver on meaty taste and looks. The next best thing, which involves putting technological triumph into reverse, is making real bacon frazzles – bits of bacon carefully cooked to look like fake bacon. We like to serve them in little greaseproof paper bags.

Serves 10–12

1KG/2¼LB RINDLESS SMOKED STREAKY BACON

VEGETABLE OIL

Take two identical oven trays and grease the top of one and the bottom of the other. Lay the strips of bacon in between and place in a hot oven (200°C/400°F/gas 6) for 20 minutes or until the bacon is cooked to crisp perfection. Blot on paper towels and carefully cut into 3cm/1 inch lengths.

SCRATCHINGS

Ask your butcher a few days in advance to set aside a nice piece of pork skin. The scratchings can be made the day before you want to serve them.

Serves 8

SKIN FROM A 2KG/4½LB PORK LOIN

SEA SALT

CASTER SUGAR

Cut your pork skin into pieces about 4 x 4cm/1½ x 1½ inches. Place the pieces on a wire rack in the sink and pour over plenty of boiling water. Leave to dry.

Sprinkle both sides with equal quantities of salt and sugar. Blast the skin in a hot oven (220°C/425°F/gas 7) for 10 minutes. Then turn the heat down to 140°C/275°F/gas 1 and continue to cook until the skin is scratchified; it will take about an hour; you'll need to drain off excess fat every 15 minutes or so.

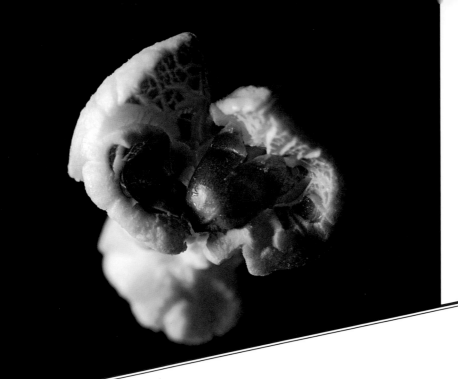

BACON POPCORN

Exotically flavoured popcorn is all over town. It's easy and inexpensive to make. Truffle-flavoured corn (add truffle oil after the corn has popped) is popular but we like bacon popcorn. We first served it to accompany a scratch 'n' sniff screening of the 1984 gothic horror movie **The Company of Wolves.**

Serves 2
50G/1¾OZ STREAKY BACON

SPLASH OF VEGETABLE OIL

100G/3½OZ POPCORN KERNELS

25G/1OZ SUGAR

Cut the bacon into small pieces and fry, with a splash of oil, in a large pan until crisp. Using a draining spoon, remove the bacon and set aside on some paper towel to drain. Leave the fat in the pan.

Add the popcorn and sugar and stir until coated. Cover with a lid and turn the heat down to low. Shake the pan every now and then until the corn has finished popping. Combine the hot popcorn with the bacon and serve.

CURRIED CRAB

This combines two Scottish greats: seafood and curry.

Serves 4
125G/4OZ WHITE CRAB MEAT
50G/1¾OZ MAYONNAISE
25G/1OZ CURRY PASTE
LEMON JUICE
CHOPPED CURLY PARSLEY, TO SERVE

For the potato cakes
250G/9OZ MASHED POTATOES
125G/4OZ FLOUR
SALT AND PEPPER
25G/1OZ BUTTER

Using a couple of forks, carefully pick through the crab to search for any stray bits of shell. Place the crab in a bowl and mix in the mayonnaise (bought is fine, and if you make your own use a neutral oil) and the curry paste. Season to taste with a squeeze of lemon juice. Refrigerate until ready to serve.

Mix the potatoes with half of the flour, beating vigorously with a wooden spoon. Season to taste with salt and pepper. Gradually incorporate more flour until the mixture starts to come away from the side of the bowl. This is easy if you use a mixer. Melt the butter in a frying pan, drop in spoonfuls of mixture and flatten with a spoon. When golden underneath, flip over and cook the other side. When cooked through, drain on paper towel and keep warm.

To assemble: spoon a neat mound of the curried crab on top of each potato cake. Top with chopped parsley.

QUAIL COTTAGE

Chicken Cottage may be the late-night supper haunt of many a seasoned drinker but our dainty Quail Cottage is much more suited to snacking while drinking.

For a bounty bucket to serve 4 to 8

8 QUAILS

½ JAR (ABOUT 180G/6OZ) MARMALADE

LEMON JUICE

VEGETABLE OIL

SALT AND PEPPER

FRESH ROSEMARY

SEASONED FLOUR

2 EGGS, BEATEN

FINE BREADCRUMBS

First, butcher your quails: with a sharp knife, remove the breasts and the legs. Remove the skin from the breasts and set the breasts and skin aside. Quail Cottage has no use for carcasses but we like to make them into a delicious soup.

For the legs: preheat the oven to 180°C/350°F/gas 4. Scrape down the tops of the legs, cutting through any sinews, so that the meat is freed from the top of the bone. In a bowl, mix half a jar of marmalade with a squeeze of lemon juice, a dash of oil, salt and pepper, and some rosemary. Add the legs and stir to coat in the mixture. Line a baking tray with foil (if you omit the foil, you'll spend hours washing up), add the marmaladey legs and roast for about 30 minutes or until golden brown. Turn and baste frequently.

For the nuggets: dip the breasts in seasoned flour, then in beaten egg and finally coat them in breadcrumbs. You can prepare these in advance. To cook, shallow fry in oil until crispy.

For the skins: deep fry in hot oil, drain on paper towel, sprinkle with salt.

To serve, pile the hot nuggets into a bowl and top with the sticky legs. Some freshly made slaw is a good accompaniment. We make ours with finely sliced carrots, red onions and fennel.

MARSHMALLOWS

Home-made marshmallows are an impressive snack. We like to flavour them with dried lavender, but you could use rose water or vanilla essence – or try your own experiments. This recipe was worked on at great length by our friend and collaborator Robin Fegen – he ended up building a forest of mallows.

Makes 100

BUTTER

PLENTY OF ICING SUGAR

20G/¾ OZ POWDERED GELATINE

125ML/4FL OZ WATER

250G/9 OZ GLUCOSE SYRUP

450G/1LB CASTER SUGAR

FOOD COLOURING (OPTIONAL)

FLAVOURING: 1 TSP VANILLA ESSENCE, ROSE WATER, DRIED LAVENDER

PINCH OF SALT

Find a baking tray about 30 x 50cm/12 x 20 inches and about 5cm/2 inches deep. Grease it really thoroughly and evenly with butter, then sift icing sugar generously and evenly over the whole thing – if there is a tiny patch without icing sugar the marshmallow will stick.

Put the gelatine and water into the bowl of a mixer and leave for 10 minutes to bloom.

Meanwhile, put the glucose syrup and caster sugar into a good-sized pan and add 60ml/4 tbsp water. Place the pan over a high heat and monitor the temperature with a sugar thermometer – heat to 240°F/115°C: this is known as the soft ball stage, meaning that if you drop a little of the very hot syrup into a jug of cold water it will form a ball that you can pick up and squeeze gently with your fingers.

Check that the gelatine has all come into contact with the water in the mixer bowl; if you like you can add several drops of food colour. Because the

marshmallow will be naturally white the colour will never get beyond pastel, so adding more than this amount of dye is probably pointless.

When the boiling sugar solution gets to 240°F/115°C, turn off the heat. Start the mixer (on the lowest speed) and carefully pour the sugar solution on to the gelatine. From this point on, you have to gradually turn the mixer up to full speed. Be careful of splashes, but the mixture thickens as it cools.

It takes up to about 10 minutes for the mallow to reach full fluffiness and stop increasing in size. At that point add your chosen flavouring, plus a pinch of salt. Continue whisking for another minute or two – taste to check the flavour. Then (if not too hot) pour into your prepared baking tray, spread evenly with a spatula and leave in a cool place for at least 16 hours.

When ready, cut up the marshmallow – dust your knife or long sharp scissors with icing sugar and sift icing sugar over every severed surface.

Suppliers

AMBERGRIS

Pure ambergris is bitchingly expensive. If you are lucky you can find your own. It's the way fortunes are made.

An excellent option is to go for natural ambergris perfume oil. It still has the smell of mystery and is arguably better for making drinks with.

Bristol Botanicals
www.bristolbotanicals.co.uk
Tel +44 (0)117 970 2100

For pure ambergris you will have to look further afield. These people will deliver "beach cast" ambergris from New Zealand.
www.ambergris.co.nz

CAFFEINE

We use food grade caffeine in a powder form, which is not available to the general public. Other types of caffeine powder are available as it is used as a sports and dietary supplement; however, we haven't tried these as an alternative.

CREAM WHIPPER

The cream whipper makes foams, helps with speedy infusion and is powered by popular dinner party drug nitrous oxide.

Cream Supplies
www.creamsupplies.co.uk
0845 226 3024
+44 (0)2392 378 700

DIETHYL ETHER

Diethyl Ether was historically a popular anaesthetic but is now mainly used as a solvent by the scientific community. It's not illegal in the UK, but is not generally available to members of the public. It is extremely volatile and highly flammable so handle with care and as per the manufacturer's instructions.

A word of warning though, if you do get hold of it, make sure what you get is pure diethyl ether. Any other derivatives and you could be in trouble. Be very careful.

GOLD

The European Union designates gold as food additive E175. You need to make sure it is over 22 carats to be food safe otherwise you'll be drinking down copper and nickel as well. You could go to a fancy art shop for it but we don't. Ours is from Leyland, the builder's supply merchant.

L. Cornelissen & Son
105 Great Russell Street
London WC1B 3RY
www.cornelissen.com
+44 (0)20 7636 1045

Leyland SDM
www.leylandsdm.co.uk
+44 (0)20 7275 2999

METHYLCELLULOSE POWDER

Methyl cellulose is a trendy chemical used by "molecular mixologists" and food experimentalists. It works as a thickener and has the unique property of setting when hot and melting when cold. It's also used to make hot non-leak pie filler in chain restaurants, as a sexual lubricant, laxative, slime in films such as *Ghostbusters* and as the jizz in pornos. Fun stuff! MSK is the place to go for rare and exotic ingredients like this; they sell it as Methocel, a gelling agent.

MSK
+44 (0)1246 412211
www.msk-ingredients.com

EMPTY PAINT TUBES

L. Cornelissen & Son
As for Gold

T N Lawrence & Son
+44 (0)1273 260280
www.lawrence.co.uk

TOBACCO

If you are going to use tobacco in cocktails, use good stuff. Black Cavendish tobacco is the blend we use, from G. Smith & Sons. They opened in 1869 so know what they are doing.

G. Smith & Sons
74 Charing Cross Road
London WC2H 0BG
http://smithsandshervs.com
+44 (0) 20 7836 7422

BIBLIOGRAPHY

Amis, Kingsley. *Everyday Drinking: The Distilled Kingsley Amis*, London: Bloomsbury, 2008.

Brillat-Savarin, Jean-Anthelme. *The Physiology of Taste*, New York: Alfred A. Knopf, 1971.

Blumenthal, Heston. *The Big Fat Duck Cookbook*, London: Bloomsbury, 2008.

Brown, Jared and Miller, Anistatia. *Spirituous Journey, A History of Drink* (Book One: From the Birth of Spirits to the Birth of the Cocktail), UK: Mixellany Limited, 2009.

Brown, Jared and Miller, Anistatia. *Spirituous Journey, A History of Drink* (Book Two: From Publicans to Master Mixologists), UK: Mixellany Limited, 2009.

Castellon, Fernando. *Larousse Cocktails*, London: Hamlyn, Octopus Publishing Group, 2005.

Cowen, Ruth. *Relish: The Extraordinary Life of Alexis Soyer*, London: Weidenfeld & Nicolson, 2006.

Craddock, Harry. *The Savoy Cocktail Book*, London: Pavilion, 1999.

Curtis, Wayne. *And a Bottle of Rum: A History of the New World in Ten Cocktails*, New York: Broadway, 2007.

Davidson, Alan. *The Oxford Companion to Food*, Oxford: Oxford University Press, 1999.

DeGroff, Dale. *The Craft of the Cocktail*, UK: Proof Publishing, 2003.

De Voto, Bernard. *The Hour: A Cocktail Manifesto*, Portland: Tin House Books, 2010.

Dickson, Paul. *Drunk: The Definitive Drinker's Dictionary*, New York: Melville House Publishing, 2009.

Edwards, John (et al.) "The influence of eating location on the acceptability of identically prepared foods." *Journal of Food Quality and Preference*, 14 (8) pp. 647-652, 2002.

Embury, David A. *The Fine Art of Mixing Drinks*, New York: Mud Puddle Books, 2008.

Faith, Nicholas. *Cognac*, London: Mitchell Beazley, 2004.

Grogan, Peter. *Grogan's Companion to Drink: the A to Z of Alcohol*, UK: Virgin Books, an imprint of Ebury Publishing, A Random House Group Company, 2010.

Henderson, Fergus. *Nose to Tail Eating*, London: Macmillan, 1999.

Horwitz, Jamie and Singley, Paulette (eds.) *Eating Architecture*, Massachusetts: Massachusetts Institute of Technology, 2004.

Van Flandern, Brian. *Vintage Cocktails*, New York: Assouline Publishing, 2009.

Kaye, Jordan and Altier, Marshall. *How to Booze: Exquisite Cocktails and Unsound Advice*, New York: Harper Collins Publishers, 2010.

Kosmas, Jason and Zaric, Dushan. *Speakeasy*, United States: Ten Speed Press, 2010.

Langan, Peter. *A Life with Food*, London: Bloomsbury, 1990.

MacDonogh, Giles. *A Palate in Revolution: Grimod de La Reynière and the Almanach des Gourmands*, London: Robin Clark, 1987.

McGee, Harold. *McGee on Food & Cooking: an Encyclopedia of Kitchen Science, History and Culture*, London: Hodder and Stoughton, 2004.

McGovern, Patrick E. *Uncorking the Past: the Quest for Wine, Beer and other Alcoholic Beverages*, London: University of California, 2009.

Robinson, Jancis. *Jancis Robinson on the Demon Drink*, London: Mitchell Beazley, 1988.

Rowley, Matthew B. *Moonshine!*, New York: Lark Books, A division of Sterling Publishing Co, Inc, 2007.

Shopsin, Kenny. *Eat Me: The Food and Philosophy of Kenny Shopsin*, New York: Knopf, 2008.

Schnakenberg, Robert. *Old Man Drinks: Recipes, Advice, and Barstool Wisdom*, Philadelphia: Quirk Books, 2010.

Thompson, Hunter S. *Fear and Loathing in Las Vegas*, London: Flamingo, 1993.

Warner, Jessica. *Craze: Gin and Debauchery in an Age of Reason*, New York: Random House, 2003.

Watman, Max. *Chasing the White Dog: An Amateur Outlaw's Adventures in Moonshine*, New York: Simon and Schuster, 2011.

Wittels, Betina J. and Hermesch, Robert. *Absinthe: Sip of Seduction*, Colorado: Speck Press, 2008.

Wondrich, David. *Punch: The Delights (and Dangers) of the Flowing Bowl*, New York: A Perigee Book (Penguin Group), 2010.

Wondrich, David. *Imbibe!*, New York: A Perigee Book (Penguin Group), 2007.

Websites

http://cookedbooks.blogspot.com (Rebecca Federman, New York Public Library culinary archive)

www.cookingissues.com (Dave Arnold, French Culinary Institute, New York)

www.ediblegeography.com (Nicola Twilley, food writer)

www.historicfood.com (Ivan Day, food historian)

www.jellymongers.co.uk

INDEX

A

A Civilization Built on Beer (2580 BC) 9
absinthe 84, 85
American Constitution (1787) 9
architectural punch bowl 100–15

B

Bacon Frazzles 149
Bacon Popcorn 150
bar snacks 146–55
bar spoon 28
Bellini 70
Black Gin Punch 108, 109
black ice 15
Black Velvet 78–80
Bloody Mary 55
Boston shaker 26–7, 31
bottle opener and corkscrew 29, 31
brandy cocktails 60–5
Buckfast 76–9
Buckie Medley 79
Home-Made Buckie 77
Bucks Fizz 70
Bullshot (A Meaty Cocktail) 118

C

Captain Fraser's Grog 92, 93
champagne cocktails 66–71
children & alcohol 90–1
chopping board 29
Citronade 114, 115
citrus squeezer 29, 30
classics 34–71
corkscrew 29, 31
cream whipper 29, 31
crushed ice 15
cubed ice 15
cures 116–25
Curried Crab 150

D

Daiquiri 48
Death in the Afternoon 69
Diana Death Jelly (1997) 8
drinking stories, our top ten 8–11

E

Eggnog 110, 111
eggs 140
Emperor's Shrub 102, 103
equipment, basic 26–31
Ether Cocktail 86, 87
Evelyn Waugh's Noonday Cocktail 118

F

Falernum 139
Fernet Branca 123
Fish House Punch 104, 105
flaming 134, 135
foams 142,143
Futurist Cocktail 114

G

galactic booze 74–5
garnishes 19, 131
Getting Drunk on the Cheap 82, 83
Gin & Tonic 36
gin cocktails 34–9
Ginger Beer 112, 113
glasses 17, 19, 130
Golden Syrup Old Fashioned 144

H

Hanky Panky 123
highballs 25
Home-Made Buckie 77
Hot Milk Posset 91

I

ice 14–15
ice bucket and ice tongs 29, 30, 31
ice cream 145
infusions 136
Ironfast 79

K

Kingsley Amis 63
Kir Royale 69
kitchen knife, paring knife, peeler, zester 29, 30, 31

L

Langan's Elixir 120, 121
Lord Byron's Boot (Late 18th Century) 8

M

Manhattan 42
Margarita 58
Marmite Black Velvet 80
marshmallows 154, 155
Martinis 22–4, 36, 37
   Provencale 136
measuring 19
Mojito 50
Moonshot 75
Moscow Mule 54
Muddler 29, 31

N

Negroni 38
Negus 90
nitrogen cavitation 138

O

Old & Obscure 88–97
Old Fashioned 24, 44, 45

P

Pickled Nelson (1805) 10
Pina Colada 51
Pink Gin 39
Pisco Sour 140, 141
Plum Sour 42–3
Poor Man's Champagne Cocktail 82
pourer 28
principles, universal cocktail 14–19
punches & party drinks 24–5, 98–115
Puss and Mew: Gin Vending Machines (early 18th Century)
   8–9

Q

Quaff for Your City! (1631) 10
Quail Cottage 152, 153

R

recipes 34–124
Royal Usquebaugh 94, 95
rum cocktails 46–51
Rum Daisy 48

S

Sabage, The Secret of 68–9
Sazerac 64, 65
scratchings 149
shaking and stirring 16
Side Car 62
sours 21–2
Soyer au Champagne 96, 97
spirit measure 27–8, 30
strainers 27, 31
sugar syrup 15–16
suppliers 156

T

tea towel and rolling pin 29, 30
techniques 126–45
tequila cocktails 56–9
Tequila Fizz 58
Tequila Sunrise 59
The Beer Flood of 1814 11
The World's Largest Punch Bowl (1694) 10–11
Tobacco Elixir 124, 125
True Friendship Punch 106, 107
types of cocktail 20–5

V

vodka cocktails 52–5

W

whisk(e)y cocktails 40–5
Whiskey Sour 43
White Cargo 145
White Monk 79
White Russian 54
Wine by the Fountain (1520) 9–10

Z

Zombie 48

HONOUR ROLL

To those who are about to drink, we salute you.

There's a horde of people who have helped us realize the cocktail dream. Parents and families who took us seriously when we turned our backs on a reasonable career in jelly to work with alcohol.

Thanks to all at Anova Books for the mind boggling hours and hot skills you have put into the project. To Nina Sharman and Georgie Hewitt who may or may not be traumatized by the experience. Your efforts have been heroic to the end. Thanks to Polly Powell for holding the faith and Maggie Ramsay for piloting the manuscript to a readable delight.

To wonder photographer Beth Evans and stylists Anna and Victoria of Lightning & Kinglyface. You are all psychic. The images you created are absolutely magical and the sort of shots we dreamt of.

Our literary agent Isabel Atherton of Creative Authors is quite simply magnificent, thank you.

The talented friends, crew and co-conspirators who have helped us realize madcap alcohol adventures on the grandest scale possible – the size of buildings. To Ann Charlott Ommedal for making B&P rock and chef Andrew Stellitano, who combines the skills of being able to cook tasty food *and* shoot it beautifully. Special thanks to Erris de Stacpoole, Alexandra Constantinides, Beth Adams, Hugo Richardson, Dom James and the unstoppable Robin Collective, inventors of the colour-changing cocktail, a drink of mystery. You guys all rule.

Our journey into alcohol has been made possible by a few noble and notable brands that have sponsored research and allowed us to experiment. Of particular note are Hendrick's Gin and the mighty Xavier Padovani, and Courvoisier with White Label. Together we've worked on some of the most epic alcohol-based installations London has seen. Pernod Absinthe, Sauza Tequila, Maker's Mark, Smirnoff Vodka, Guinness, Martini, Bacardi Rum, Fever-Tree and Glenfiddich all pitched in for the book.

To everyone that visits our installations and drinks what we make. You've been the unwilling participants in a grand experiment. This book is the result so we are eternally grateful.

To Ivan Day, our inspiration and food idol.

If your name's not here it's because the list to thank gets longer with each project. It's now far greater than cocktail-drinking men can remember. Your help is humbling and we offer our sincerest apologies.

Finally to our girlfriends who have tolerated our long nights of "research" and who are the first to be drafted in to help on any project, no matter how bizarre. To Harry's girlfriend Cecilia Carey, who has spent days spraying half a tonne of sugar onto our exploding cake, and Sam's girlfriend Emma Rios, who most recently illustrated the Celestial Bed where people made love in the Museum of London. If we can get through projects like that together we can get through anything.

Now we're going to binge drink until we pass out.

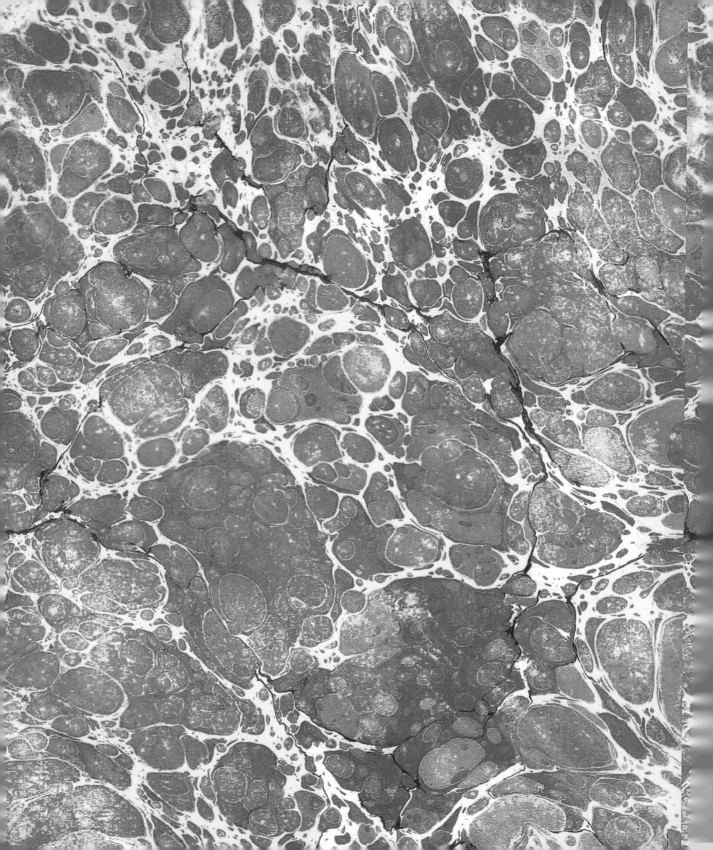